QUICK PREP

Obtaining a US Visa
Based on Achievement
What You Need to Know

Brian H. Getson

For additional copies or customer service inquiries, please e-mail west.customer.service@thomson.com.

ISBN 978-0-314-29203-2

Mat #41653476

ACKNOWLEDGMENT

I would like to thank my wife Jessica, my children Henry, Ben and Claire, and my mother Judy for their support in my career and in the writing of this book.

DEDICATION

This book is dedicated to the memory of my father, Allan Getson, who inspired me to join the legal profession and who gave me the opportunity to become a successful immigration attorney.

CONTENTS

Introduction

The United States is a country of great opportunity. Individuals around the world have been pursuing the American Dream for hundreds of years. However, it is not possible for everyone who wants to live and work in the United States, either permanently or temporarily, to obtain legal work authorization. The US immigration laws restrict the ability of an individual to work in the United States based both on the nature of the proposed work and the qualifications of the individual.

There are special provisions under the US immigration laws for individuals with recognized talent in certain qualifying fields, i.e., those with a proven record of achievement, to obtain authorization to work in the United States, either permanently or temporarily.

It is necessary for such individuals to establish via tangible evidence that they meet the high standards of proven achievement required under the US immigration laws and that they will be coming to the United States to work in their field of endeavor. The standards one must meet to obtain work authorization based on achievement are set forth in both the United States Immigration & Nationality Act enacted by the US Congress and the Regulations promulgated by United States Citizenship and Immigration Services (USCIS). The general provisions of immigration laws enacted by Congress in the United States Immigration and Nationality Act are interpreted and implemented by regulations issued by various agencies, including USCIS. These regulations apply the law to individual situations. After regulations are published in the *Federal Register*, they are collected and published in the Code of Federal Regulations, commonly referred to as the CFR. The CFR is arranged by subject title and generally parallels the structure of the United States Code. Title 8 of the CFR deals with "Aliens and Nationality," as does Title 8 of the United States Code.

Documenting that a foreign national actually meets the standards for achievement set forth in the United States Immigration & Nationality Act and Regulations in Title 8 of the CFR can be challenging. USCIS is the government agency that determines whether an individual meets the high level of achievement required to obtain the right to work in the United States in the relevant employment-based categories. USCIS can be very strict in evaluating evidence of achievement and interpreting the regulations. It is therefore imperative for foreign nationals to thoroughly understand both the legal standards of the category in which a petition for permanent or temporary work authorization is being made and the type of evidence that should be submitted to USCIS in support of a petition. Additionally, the United States wants to ensure that an individual who establishes a proven record of achievement in a field is going to continue working in that field to benefit the United States if given authorization to work in the United States. The United States is not going to grant a Nobel Prize winner a nonimmigrant (temporary) or immigrant (permanent) visa to work at McDonald's!

A nonimmigrant visa is a visa issued to individuals with a permanent residence outside the United States who would like to be in the United States on a temporary basis, such as for work. All nonimmigrant work visas require an employer sponsor and require that the individual only work for the employer sponsor. An immigrant visa is the visa issued to individuals wishing to live permanently in the United States. Most immigrant visas based on employment also require an employer sponsor but certain employment-based immigrant visa categories allow a foreign national with documented accomplishments in his or her field of endeavor to "self-file" an immigrant petition.

Scientific researchers are the primary class of individuals who utilize the "achievement-based" immigrant and nonimmigrant work visas. However, individuals with accomplishments in fields such as business, athletics, education, and the arts are also eligible to apply for work visas based on achievement. The author has obtained immigrant/nonimmigrant visas for scientific researchers as well as individuals with achievement in diverse fields such as an Olympic tennis coach, a disc jockey, an economist, and a racehorse trainer.

The three most widely used immigrant visa subcategories created by Congress for individuals to obtain a green card based on achievement are: 1) employment-based first preference (EB-1A): extraordinary ability aliens, 2) employment-based first preference (EB-1B): outstanding professors and researchers, and 3) employment-based second preference (EB-2): national interest waiver.

1) EB-1A extraordinary ability aliens (self-filing is permitted):

   Must establish you are among the small percentage at the very top of your field.

2) EB-1B outstanding professors and researchers (requires employer sponsorship for a tenured/tenure-track position or a permanent research position):

   Must establish you have received international recognition as outstanding for your accomplishments.

3) EB-2 national interest waiver (self-filing is permitted):

   Must establish your accomplishments have had a degree of influence on your field as a whole above and beyond the substantial majority of others.

Congress also created two nonimmigrant visa categories based on achievement for temporary entrance into the United States for employment: 1) O-1 visa: extraordinary ability aliens, and 2) P visa: athletes, artists, and entertainers.

Achievement-Based Immigrant Categories for Permanent Residence

Ordinarily, for a foreign national to obtain permanent residence (i.e., a green card) through employment, the foreign national must receive a full-time job offer from a United States employer at a required minimum wage known as the prevailing wage and the prospective employer must file a PERM Labor Certification Application, which seeks certification from the United States Department of Labor that there are no ready, willing, qualified, and available United States workers for the position. Prior to filing a PERM Labor Certification Application the prospective employer must follow specific recruitment steps mandated by the United States Department of Labor to determine United States worker availability. The PERM Labor Certification Application can only be filed if the recruitment fails to yield a ready, willing, qualified, and available United States worker for the position. Thus, for most foreign nationals, a green card through employment is only possible with a specific job offer at a specific wage and a clear demonstration of the lack of a United States worker following a specific type of mandated recruitment.

For individuals who meet the required standard of achievement in a certain field, they can obtain a green card based on their achievement without regard to United States worker availability and without regard to a specific wage. For many individuals who meet the required standard of achievement in a certain field, a green card is also possible without regard to a specific employer sponsor. Individuals filing as extraordinary ability aliens, outstanding professors and researchers, or for a national interest waiver can skip the PERM Labor Certification process altogether and individuals filing as extraordinary ability aliens or for a national interest waiver can self-file without the need for an employer sponsor. These are major advantages over the traditional PERM Labor Certification process and why anyone who may qualify for an achievement-based green card category should attempt to file in one of these categories prior to undertaking the PERM Labor Certification process. If an achievement-based green card application is denied, a PERM Labor Certification could always be filed as a backup.

Another major advantage of the two employment-based first preference categories of EB-1A extraordinary ability aliens and EB-1B outstanding professors and researchers applies to foreign nationals from China and India. There is an overall numerical limit for permanent employment-based immigrants. Additionally, under the current law, each country is limited to a certain percentage of the worldwide level of United States immigrant admissions, otherwise known as per-country limits. A percentage of the total visas are equally allocated to the first, second, and third preference categories (plus certain unused numbers) and the remaining visas are allocated to the fourth and fifth preference categories. Because of the numerical and per-country limits placed on permanent employment-based visas, the waiting time to be eligible to apply for an employment-based green card can be lengthy. This is especially true for foreign nationals from China and India as the number of individuals from these two countries who seek employment-based green cards in the most widely used preference categories exceeds the per-country limits. However, because so few individuals worldwide (including from China and India) meet the eligibility requirements for EB-1A extraordinary ability aliens or EB-1B outstanding professors and researchers, there is almost never a wait for foreign nationals from China or India to apply for a green card in the first preference category. Therefore, potentially qualified foreign nationals from China or India generally file for EB-1A or EB-1B (with EB-2 as a backup) as there is no wait to apply for a green card if a petition is approved in one of these first preference categories. There is a wait of several years for foreign nationals from China or India to apply for a green card if a petition is approved in the second preference EB-2 national interest waiver category.

Foreign nationals from every country in the world other than China and India generally only self-file in the EB-2 national interest waiver category as the legal standard for approval is more favorable than EB-1A extraordinary ability aliens or EB-1B outstanding professors and researchers and there is usually no wait to apply for a green card if an EB-2 national interest waiver petition is approved for a foreign national born anywhere other than China or India.

In the EB-2 national interest waiver category, USCIS has initiated an entrepreneur in residence initiative and a foreign national with certain achievement in business could benefit from the USCIS focus on entrepreneurs and startup companies to obtain a green card in this category.

The initial step in the process of petitioning for permanent residence in an achievement-based employment category is the filing of Form I-140 immigrant petition for alien worker and supporting documents with USCIS. The date of filing of the I-140 petition is known as the priority date. The EB-1A extraordinary ability aliens and EB-1B outstanding professors and researchers categories allow for premium processing service of the I-140 petition, which means that for an extra fee, USCIS will decide the I-140 petition in fifteen days or less by issuing an approval, denial, request for additional evidence, or notice of intent to deny. If an individual is outside the United States, on approval of the I-140 petition, the case will be sent to the United States Department of State National Visa Center and when the priority date is current, the paperwork can be completed to arrange for an immigrant visa interview at the United States embassy in the country where the foreign national resides. For individuals in the United States, they can either elect to apply for an immigrant visa at the United States embassy in their home country (which is rarely done) or, if they meet the eligibility requirements, they can apply for permanent residence from within the United States in a process known as adjustment of status, which involves filing an I-485 application for adjustment of status with supporting documents. If the priority date is current, the option exists to file the I-485 application simultaneously with the I-140 petition. However, since the standards for approval are high for all of the achievement-based employment categories, most foreign nationals choose to wait for approval of the I-140 petition prior to filing the I-485 application.

Achievement-Based Nonimmigrant Categories for Temporary Employment

The two achievement-based nonimmigrant visa categories are O-1 and P.

The O-1 visa is a temporary work visa available to those foreign nationals who have "extraordinary ability." The O-1A visa is for individuals who have demonstrated extraordinary ability/achievement in the arts, sciences, education, business, or athletics. USCIS interprets the statute very broadly to encompass most fields of creative endeavor. For example, chefs, carpenters, and lecturers can all obtain O-1A visas. The O-1B visa is for individuals who have demonstrated extraordinary ability/achievement in the motion picture, television, or music industry. The foreign national entering the United States must be coming to work in their field of ability, but the position need not require the services of a person of extraordinary ability.

Before a person will be granted an O-1 visa, USCIS requires a consultation with a United States-based organization. An O-1 petition must include an advisory opinion from a peer group, labor union, or person with expertise in the foreign national's field. This opinion can state simply that the group has no objection to issuing the visa, or can detail the foreign national's achievements. If the achievements are detailed, the letter should also address the foreign national's ability and the nature of the position offered. Consultation for an individual of extraordinary ability in the field of arts is waived in those instances where the foreign national seeks readmission to the United States to perform similar services within two years of the date of a previous consultation.

Form I-129 petition for a nonimmigrant worker is used to petition for the O-1 visa for a nonimmigrant worker. This must be submitted along with the consultation opinion, evidence documenting the foreign national's extraordinary ability, and details of the proposed work in the United States. The petition is to be approved for the duration of the event in which the foreign national will participate, for a maximum of three years.

An O-1 visa may be extended in one-year increments for an indefinite period. Form I-129 is also used to file for an extension.

O-1 visas are considered "dual intent visas," meaning that even though the foreign national has filed for permanent resident status based on a a PERM Labor Certification Application or petition for classification as a preference worker leading to permanent residence, the O-1 visa cannot be denied.

The P visa is generally used by foreign nationals in athletics or the entertainment industry who do not meet the extraordinary ability standards of an O-1 visa.

The P visa is divided into five categories:

1) The P-1A visa is for a foreign national coming temporarily to perform at a specific athletic competition as an individual or as part of a team participating at an internationally recognized level of performance;

2) The P-1B visa is for a foreign national entertainer, coming
    temporarily to perform as a member of a foreign-based
    entertainment group that has been recognized internationally as
    outstanding in the discipline for a significant period and who has
    sustained a relationship (usually for one year) with the group;

3) The P-2 visa is for a foreign national coming temporarily to perform
    as an artist or entertainer, individually or as part of a group, under a
    reciprocal exchange program between an organization in the United
    States and an organization in another country;

4) The P-3 visa is for a foreign national who is coming temporarily
    to perform, teach, or coach, individually or as part of a group, in
    the arts or entertainment fields in a program that is culturally
    unique; and

5) The P-1S, P-2S, or P-3S visa is for essential support personnel
    who are highly skilled foreign nationals coming temporarily as
    an essential and integral part of the competition or performance
    of a principal P-1, P-2, or P-3 or because they perform support
    services that are essential to the successful performance of the P-
    1, P-2, or P-3.

In reality, P visas are most often used for athletes and entertainers who
perform as part of a team or entertainment group for trips of limited
duration, such as a concert tour or a sports season. In that the P-1 visa is
employer-specific, P-1 athletes and entertainers who are members of a
team or group may not perform work or services separate and apart from
the team or entertainment group during their P-1 time.

Like the O-1 visa, the United States employer must file Form I-129 with
supporting documents including a consultation from an appropriate labor
organization. The consultation must describe the work or services to be
performed in the United States and the foreign national's qualifications
for such work. If no appropriate labor organization exists, this
requirement is excused. An individual may be admitted in P-1 status for
as much time as is approved for the subject competition, event, or
performance. If a foreign national is admitted on a P-1 visa as an
individual athlete, the period of initial status may be any length of time
but not more than five years, and that period of time may be extended for
a period of up to five years.

For both the O and P visas, if the individual is outside the United States, on approval of the I-129 petition by USCIS, the individual will apply for a nonimmigrant visa at the United States embassy in their country of residence. Upon issuance of the nonimmigrant visa, the individual will enter the United States and receive an I-94 card, which authorizes employment with the sponsoring employer. If the individual is in the United States in another valid nonimmigrant status, if eligible to do so, a change of status to O or P can be accomplished from within the United States. Extensions of status can also be applied for from within the United States. Premium processing is available for both O and P visas and a determination must be made in each individual case whether premium processing is worthwhile. Guidance is provided herein to help answer questions about expediting the processing of a petition and whether a faster processing time is worth the extra cost.

Individual chapters in this book guide foreign nationals on the legal standards of the immigrant categories of EB-1A extraordinary ability aliens, EB-1B outstanding professors and researchers, and EB-2 national interest waiver and the nonimmigrant categories of O-1 extraordinary ability aliens and P-1 athletes, artists, and entertainers. Guidance on the type of evidence to submit in support of a petition in the respective categories, including reference letters, is also provided. Finally, the importance of the cover letter to USCIS in support of a petition is emphasized.

1

EB-1A Extraordinary Ability Aliens

The EB-1A extraordinary ability aliens category covers foreign nationals with extraordinary ability in the sciences, arts, education, business, or athletics. Individuals must demonstrate that they have sustained national or international acclaim and that their achievements have been recognized in the field of expertise, indicating that they are one of that small percentage who has risen to the very top of their field of endeavor. They must plan to continue to work in their area of extraordinary ability and must substantially benefit prospectively the United States.

The extraordinary ability aliens category does not require an employer sponsor. This means that the foreign national may self-file a petition rather than needing an employer to file a petition.

In the case of an employer sponsoring the foreign national and signing the Form I-140 immigrant petition for alien worker, an offer of employment consisting of an employment letter or contract would be submitted.

In the case of a foreign national self-filing by independently signing the Form I-140 immigrant petition for alien worker, the extraordinary ability aliens category requires "clear evidence" that the foreign national is coming to the United States to work in the area of expertise. For an individual already in the United States working in the area of expertise in a nonimmigrant status such as H-1B or O-1 who intends to continue working for the nonimmigrant employer, this requirement is typically met by the individual providing a statement detailing plans to continue working for the nonimmigrant employer upon receipt of United States permanent resident status with an indication of intent to work in the same field of endeavor if a change of employer were to occur in the future. In a situation where the foreign national is applying from outside the United States or is in the United States in a nonimmigrant status but is not working, this requirement is typically met by the individual providing letter(s) from prospective employer(s) or evidence of prearranged commitments such as contracts.

Nearly everyone self-files in the extraordinary ability aliens category to obviate the need for employer involvement. However, in certain cases having an employer sponsor could help prove that the foreign national is of extraordinary ability and/or help prove the foreign national's plans to continue working in the field of endeavor. In that an EB-1A petition may be filed by the foreign national or anyone on behalf of the foreign national, an approved EB-1A petition remains valid where the petition was filed by a prospective employer but the foreign national subsequently intends to pursue different employment in the field. In such a case the foreign national would be required to present to USCIS new evidence of the intent to continue working in the field of endeavor.

The foreign national must also indicate that his or her entry will substantially benefit the United States. Evidence that may be submitted to satisfy this requirement includes, but is not limited to, letters from current or prospective employers or individuals who work in the field, other evidence explaining how the work will be advantageous and of use to the interests of the United States on a national level, or a statement from the foreign national detailing plans on how his or her work will substantially benefit, prospectively, the United States. This is generally addressed in the statement detailing plans for work and the reference letters and therefore usually does not require particular evidence.

The regulations define extraordinary ability as a level of expertise indicating that the individual is one of those few who have risen to the very top of the field of endeavor. The starting point in preparing an extraordinary ability alien petition is thus to define the field of endeavor.

There is great flexibility in defining the field of endeavor. It is usually best to show that the foreign national is a "big fish in a small pond" by comparing the foreign national to others in a specialized field as it may be difficult to show a foreign national is one of the small percentage of researchers at the very top of a very general field like cancer research or cell biology. Some examples of specialized fields used in extraordinary ability petitions of the author's clients include "synthetic medicinal chemistry," "human monoclonal antibody therapeutics," "determining the underlying molecular mechanisms of lung biology in an effort to find treatments for respiratory diseases," and "the development of biomedical devices for ophthalmology." However, a foreign national with accomplishments in multiple specialty fields within a broader discipline may be better served by comparison to others in the broader discipline to incorporate all of the foreign national's accomplishments within the "field."

Under the regulations there are two ways to establish the sustained national or international acclaim necessary to demonstrate extraordinary ability. First, the foreign national can show receipt of a one-time achievement (that is, a major, internationally recognized award) such as a Nobel Prize or an Academy Award. Barring the receipt of such an award, the second, and more common method, is for the foreign national to document three of the following ten types of evidence:

- Receipt of lesser nationally or internationally recognized prizes or awards for excellence in the field of endeavor
- Membership in associations in the field of endeavor that require outstanding achievements of their members as judged by recognized national or international experts
- Published material about the foreign national and his or her work in professional journals, major trade publications, or major media relating to the work of the foreign national in the field
- Participation, either individually or on a panel, as a judge of others in the same or an allied field
- Original scientific, scholarly, artistic, athletic, or business-related contributions of major significance in the field of endeavor
- Authorship of scholarly articles in the field, published in professional or major trade publications or major media
- Display of the foreign national's work at artistic exhibitions or showcases

- Performance in a leading or critical role for organizations or establishments that have a distinguished reputation
- Commanding a high salary/remuneration compared to others in the field
- Commercial success in the performing arts as shown by box office receipts or music/video sales

As these ten categories of evidence do not encompass all the evidence that could be presented to show extraordinary ability, there is also a catch-all category allowing submission of other comparable evidence.

In addition to receiving a one-time achievement or meeting three out of the ten requirements with regard to the above categories of evidence, per the federal court case *Kazarian v. USCIS*, it is necessary for the foreign national to show by a preponderance of the evidence that he or she is among the small percentage at the very top of the field.[1]

USCIS thus conducts a two-part test to determine whether someone is an individual of extraordinary ability:

- First, USCIS determines whether the individual has submitted evidence to show that he or she:

  o Has received a one-time achievement (a major internationally recognized award); or,
  o Qualifies under at least three of the ten criteria required for this classification.

- Second, if the individual establishes receipt of a one-time achievement (a major internationally recognized award), or meets at least three of the other criteria, USCIS then determines whether the individual has submitted evidence demonstrating that he or she:

  o Has sustained national or international acclaim. In determining whether the individual has enjoyed "sustained" national or

---

[1] *Kazarian v. U.S. Citizenship & Immigration Servs.*, 596 F.3d 1115 (9th Cir. 2010).

international acclaim, such acclaim must be maintained. In other words, it is not acceptable for an individual to have achieved extraordinary ability in the past but then failed to maintain a comparable level of acclaim thereafter and,

o Has achievements that have been recognized in the field of expertise, indicating that the individual is one of that small percentage who has risen to the very top of the field of endeavor.

The documentary evidence needed to satisfy each category is stringent. The preparation of evidence is a long and careful process. Submitting proper evidence is necessary to convince USCIS that the foreign national meets the requirements for approval as an extraordinary ability alien. Submitting the wrong kind of evidence, or stretching to meet a category in which the foreign national is clearly not qualified, weakens the overall argument that the foreign national meets the requirements for approval as an extraordinary ability alien. It usually takes my clients and me approximately three to six months to effectively prepare an EB-1A extraordinary ability aliens petition.

Part One of the Extraordinary Ability Aliens Analysis

Documenting a one-time achievement that is a major internationally recognized award is self-explanatory and the following evidence about the award should be submitted:

- That the award is internationally recognized in the field as one of the top awards for the field;
- The criteria used to grant the award;
- The significance of the award in the field;
- The reputation of the organization or the panel granting the award;
- Documentation of previous winners of the award who enjoyed international acclaim at the time of receiving the award; and,
- That the award attracts competition from internationally recognized individuals in the field.

Ninety-nine percent of all foreign nationals applying in the extraordinary ability aliens category do not have such a one-time achievement and therefore look to meet the requirements via documentary evidence in three of the ten enumerated categories. The following is typical of what USCIS requires to satisfy the extraordinary ability aliens categories:

Receipt of Lesser National or International Prizes or Awards for Excellence in the Field of Endeavor

Any prizes or awards submitted in support of an extraordinary ability aliens petition must be national or international, must be competitive prizes or awards, and must be prizes or awards given based on outstanding achievement.

Prizes or awards given to students or early career professionals in the field inherently exclude established professionals who have already achieved excellence in the field of endeavor and therefore such honors are generally not considered by USCIS to be nationally or internationally recognized prizes or awards for excellence in the field of endeavor. For example, a "Young Investigator" award is generally given to students or early professionals in the field and inherently excludes established professionals who have already achieved excellence the field. Such an award should generally not be submitted in support of this category of an extraordinary ability aliens petition as it could diminish the overall argument. Instead, such an award can be utilized in support of satisfying the category of original contributions of major significance.

For any prize or award submitted, the following should be provided:

- A copy of each prize or award certificate; or
- A clear photograph of each prize or award; or
- Public announcement regarding the awarding of the prizes or awards issued by the granting organization.

Additionally, it is necessary to provide documentation that the prize or award is national/international, that it is competitive, and what the criteria is to receive the prize or award.

The following should be provided in addition to proof of the foreign national actually receiving the award:

- The criteria used to give the prizes or awards
- Information on the reputation of the organization granting the prizes or awards
- Documentary evidence demonstrating:

    o The significance of the prizes or awards, to include the national or international recognition the prizes or awards share;
    o The reputation of the organization granting the prizes or awards;
    o Who is considered for the prizes or awards, including the geographic scope for which candidates may apply;
    o How many prizes or awards are awarded each year;
    o Previous winners who enjoy national or international acclaim; and

- Documentary evidence establishing how the prizes or awards were given for excellence in the field.

The foreign national may also submit any other information about the prizes or awards that would help establish that the prizes or awards should be considered by USCIS to be nationally or internationally recognized prizes or awards for excellence in the field of endeavor.

Foreign nationals should keep in mind that the plain language of this category clearly states and requires documentation of the foreign national's receipt of lesser nationally or internationally recognized prizes (plural) or awards (plural) for excellence in the field. If the foreign national has received only one prize or award the foreign national should not attempt to meet this category but rather should use the prize or award in support of satisfying the category of original contributions of major significance.

Membership in Associations in the Field of Endeavor That Require Outstanding Achievements of its Members as Judged by Recognized National or International Experts

The plain language of this criterion states that the association must require outstanding achievements of its members as judged by recognized national or international experts in their disciplines or fields. The evidence must show that the basis for granting memberships in the submitted associations was outstanding achievements in the field of endeavor as judged by recognized national or international experts in the field.

To satisfy this criterion the following documents may be submitted:

- A copy of the foreign national's membership certificate, a letter from the organization granting membership, or an Internet printout of the list of members including the foreign national.
- Information to establish that the individuals who review prospective members' applications are recognized as national or international experts in their disciplines or fields. This is generally obtained by finding the list of membership committee members of an association on the Internet and printing out documentation regarding their credentials.
- The section of the association's constitution or bylaws that discusses the qualifications required of the reviewers on the review panel of the association.
- The section of the association's constitution or bylaws that discusses the criteria for membership for the foreign national's level of membership in the association.
- Evidence that describes the association's goals, mission, or target membership. It is important to recognize the difference between membership in associations where anyone in the field can become a member and membership in associations that require outstanding achievement.

Examples of associations where anyone can become a member and therefore membership is not helpful to an extraordinary ability aliens petition include:

- The American Association for the Advancement of Science: Membership is open to all individuals who support the goals and objectives of the Association and are willing to contribute to the achievement of those goals and objectives.
- Society for Neuroscience: Scientists who have done research relating to neuroscience are eligible for regular membership

- American Chemical Society: Regular membership is for a person who has a degree or certification in chemical or related sciences, or certification as a teacher of a chemical science.

Examples of associations in which membership requires outstanding achievements as judged by recognized national or international experts and therefore membership can be used to meet the criterion for an extraordinary ability aliens petition include:

- American Association for Cancer Research: Active membership is open to investigators worldwide. Individuals who have conducted two years of research resulting in peer-reviewed publications relevant to cancer and cancer-related biomedical science, or who have made substantial contributions to cancer research in an administrative or educational capacity, are eligible. Evidence of patents relevant to cancer research may be provided as qualifications for membership in lieu of peer-reviewed publications.
- The American Association of Immunologists: Active regular membership is available to those worldwide who have a strong interest in and have made a substantial contribution to the field of immunology. To be eligible, a candidate must possess a PhD or equivalent graduate degree in immunology or a related discipline and be an author of one publication on an immunological topic.
- Society of Toxicology: Qualified persons who have a continuing professional interest in toxicology and (a) who have conducted and published original research in some phase of toxicology or (b) who are generally recognized as expert in some phase of toxicology shall be eligible for full membership.
- American Society of Pharmacology and Experimental Therapeutics: Any qualified investigator who has conducted and published a meritorious original investigation in pharmacology shall be eligible for membership in the Society.

It is necessary to document both the criteria for membership in the association and that applications for membership in the association are judged by recognized national or international experts in their disciplines or fields.

Foreign nationals should keep in mind that the plain language of this category clearly requires documentation of membership in associations (plural) in the field that requires outstanding achievements of their members, as judged by recognized national or international experts in their disciplines or fields. If the foreign national is a member of only one such association the foreign national should not attempt to meet this category but rather should use the membership in support of satisfying the category of original contributions of major significance.

Published Material about the Foreign National and His or Her Work in Professional Journals, Major Trade Publications, or Major Media

The plain language of this criterion clearly requires that the published material be about the foreign national and relate to the foreign national's work. Citation to the foreign national's work in other articles does not satisfy this criterion. Citations are a measure of influence that the foreign national's work has had on the field and should be addressed under the separate category of original contributions of major significance. Citations to the foreign national's work are not published material about the foreign national under this category.

The most commonly utilized evidence under this category is where the foreign national's work has been discussed in major media. For example, if a scientific researcher has made a groundbreaking original scientific contribution of major significance such a finding will often be disseminated to the public via discussion in articles written about the finding in multiple major media outlets. Other examples include review articles, editorials or book chapters written primarily about the foreign national's research.

For extraordinary ability aliens who are not scientific researchers such as athletes, actors, authors, etc., there is often discussion in major media about the individuals' accomplishments.

The author typically provides the following documentation in support of this category:

- A printout of any media articles that discuss the foreign national's work such as from NewsRX, Science Daily, etc.
- Copies of any review articles, editorials, and/or book chapters that primarily discuss the foreign national's work along with information about the professional publication in which the discussion appears
- Articles in any major trade publications about the foreign national along with information about the trade organization.

The evidence must indicate that the published material was in professional or major trade publications or other major media. Again, USCIS takes the position that having one's work citied in various journals does not meet this criterion, since the material is not primarily about the foreign national's work but rather a reference to that work. In other words, unevaluated listings in a subject matter index or footnote, or reference to the foreign national's work without evaluation are insufficient. Articles submitted in support of this category must be about the foreign national's work, not about the work of those that authored the articles.

It is important to set forth that the publications qualify as professional or major trade publications or other major media. The evidence should show that the articles are primarily about the foreign national's work that was discussed in professional or major trade publications or other major media.

Documentary evidence should include:

- The title, date, and author of the published material;
- The circulation (online and/or in print); and
- The intended audience of the publication.

The evidence submitted should be specific to the media format in which it was published. If the material was published online, the evidence should relate to the website. If it was published in print, the evidence should relate to the printed publication.

The published material should be about the foreign national's work in the field, not just about the foreign national's employer or other organizations with which the foreign national is associated. Furthermore, marketing materials created to sell the foreign national's products or to promote the foreign national's services are not generally considered published material about the foreign national.

Participation, Either Individually or on a Panel, as a Judge of Others in the Same or an Allied Field

For most foreign nationals, meeting this criterion involves judging the work of others as a peer-reviewer reviewing manuscripts submitted for publication to international scientific journals.

To document judging the work of others, the author typically submits a letter from the journal describing the journal, describing the criterion to be invited as a peer-reviewer, describing why the foreign national was invited as a peer-reviewer based on accomplishments, and describing the review activity conducted by the foreign national. The letter should indicate that the foreign national was selected based on intimate knowledge of the foreign national's accomplishments in the field as opposed to the editors of the journal only being aware of the foreign national's work in a broader context.

The author also provides the e-mail correspondence between the journal and the foreign national for each review conducted including the e-mail inviting the foreign national to conduct the review, the e-mail from the foreign national agreeing to conduct the review, the e-mail from the foreign national containing the actual review, and the e-mail from the journal thanking the foreign national for conducting the actual review.

There are other ways a foreign national can judge the work of others, such as determining awards at a research symposium, judging a talent show (i.e., Simon Cowell as a judge on *American Idol*), and so on. Regardless of the type of judging conducted, the evidence should document that the judging actually occurred and what the criteria was for the foreign national to be selected as a judge.

Original Scientific or Scholarly Contributions of Major Significance in the Field of Endeavor

This is the most open-ended of the extraordinary ability aliens criterion. USCIS is looking for objective documentary evidence of the major significance of original scientific or scholarly contributions to the field.

The primary means to demonstrate original scientific or scholarly contributions of major significance in the field of endeavor is through reference letters from independent experts in the field and supervisors. The reference letters serve as evidence that people throughout the field currently consider the work important. Other types of evidence that can be provided to meet this criterion include presentations made at international conferences, citations to the foreign national's work, patents and any royalty payments made on the patents, a discovery being implemented by others, such as in clinical practice, industry, and so on, drug development by pharmaceutical companies, and the importance of the accomplishments to other United States government agencies.

Evidence of work implemented by others can include:

- Contracts with companies using the discovery and/or letters from companies regarding the use of the discovery;
- Licensed technology being used by others;
- Patents currently being utilized and shown to be significant to the field. This is generally evidenced by providing copies of the patents and letter(s) regarding the nature and significance of the patents. Evidence of royalty payments on patents is strong evidence of original scientific contributions of major significance. USCIS also considers as important evidence that a major significant contribution has provoked widespread public commentary in the field or has been widely cited. It is not uncommon for research to be considered first time discoveries, to be helpful in furthering future research, and to be published in notable journals. Research that has been heavily cited and/or widely implemented is indicative of research that has made a major significant contribution.

- To support this the author provides a citation list from Google Scholar, Web of Science, etc., along with approximately twenty to twenty-five of the best articles that cite the foreign national's work by providing a copy of the first page of the article, the page(s) of the article that discusses the foreign national's work with said discussion highlighted, and the reference page of the article with said reference(s) highlighted. It should be noted that self-citation does not demonstrate impact of the foreign national's work on the field as a whole.
- Letters from individuals who have utilized the foreign national's work in the course of their own work, indicating how they utilized the work of the foreign national, how they discussed it, and why it is significant, demonstrate how citation to the work is reflective of the foreign national's influence. Additionally, if an individual could not have performed their own work without the benefit of the work of the foreign national that should be highlighted.

It is necessary to document that the foreign national's contributions were "original" (not merely replicating the work of others) and were of "major" significance to the field of endeavor. The reference letters are the primary means of documenting original contributions of major significance to the field and must establish that the accomplishments represent major original accomplishments and have made a major significant impact. USCIS certainly evaluates statements submitted as expert testimony and considers whether such statements support eligibility for the foreign national having made original contributions of major significance. Letters from United States governmental agencies such as the United States Food and Drug Administration or United States Centers for Disease Control and Prevention can assist in persuading USCIS that original contributions to the field are of "major significance." While the submission of letters from experts in the field carry weight with USCIS, such letters alone cannot form the cornerstone of a successful claim of national/international recognition.

For scientific researchers, conducting research and making first time discoveries is inherent to the nature of the position. In that reference letters are not presumptive evidence of eligibility, the foreign national should provide evidence beyond reference letters in support of this category. The evidence must demonstrate that the research findings are more than just helpful, have actually made a major significant impact within the field, and have enjoyed a larger following. Showing that other researchers have emulated the foreign national's techniques or have applied the foreign national's research results evidence that contributions are not only original but are also of major significance to the field. The evidence must demonstrate that the foreign national's field has changed as a result of the foreign national's work beyond the incremental improvements in knowledge and understanding expected from valid original research. It must be shown that the totality of the foreign national's work, as demonstrated by preexisting, independent and objective evidence, has risen to a major significance within the field.

Furthermore, the foreign national's accomplishments must represent original contributions of major significance to the field as of the filing date of the I-140 petition.

Authorship of Scholarly Articles in the Field, Published in Professional or Major Trade Publications or Media.

This is the most straightforward of the extraordinary ability aliens criterion. A scholarly article is one that is written for learned persons in a given field. "Learned" is defined by USCIS as "having or demonstrating profound knowledge or scholarship." Learned persons include all persons having profound knowledge of a field.

The foreign national should provide copies of the first page of any publication he or she authored in any professional or major trade publication. These are usually peer-reviewed international scientific journals. For any publication in major media, a copy of the entire published article should be provided.

Publications should be provided even if the foreign national was not the first author and even if the publication was in a national or regional journal or trade publication as opposed to one with international circulation.

In addition to providing a copy of the publication itself, background information about the journal/publication/media should be provided. For example, if the foreign national published an article in *Nature*, information about that journal should be printed from the Internet and provided to USCIS to document that *Nature* is a professional publication.

Display of the Foreign National's Work at Artistic Exhibitions or Showcases

This criterion is limited to an artist who is seeking to qualify as an extraordinary ability alien. The evidence should establish that the work product displayed at the artistic exhibition or showcase belongs to the foreign national and that the venue(s) (virtual or otherwise) where the work product was displayed were artistic exhibitions or showcases.

To show that the work displayed was created by the foreign national, the following may be submitted:

- Evidence that the work was primarily created by the foreign national
- Materials created to promote the foreign national's artistic works
- Sales records listing the foreign national as the creator of the sold works

To show that the venues where the foreign national's work has been displayed qualify as artistic exhibitions or showcases, the following may be submitted:

- Evidence that the venue(s) (virtual or otherwise) where the foreign national's work was displayed were artistic exhibitions or showcases
- Materials created to promote and publicize the artistic exhibitions or showcases

Performance in a Leading or Critical Role for Organizations or Establishments That Have a Distinguished Reputation

This criterion is typically met by providing a letter from an organization or establishment discussing the leading or critical role played by the foreign national relative to others employed at the organization or establishment and by providing evidence of the distinguished reputation of the organization or establishment either within the context of the letter or through independent corroborating evidence. A distinguished reputation means the organization or establishment is one of eminence, distinction, or excellence.

The letter should be provided by an individual with personal knowledge of the significance of the foreign national's leading or critical role. The letter should contain detailed and probative information that specifically addresses how the foreign national's role for the organization or establishment is or was leading or critical. Details should include the specific tasks or accomplishments of the foreign national as compared to others who are employed in similar pursuits within the field of endeavor. For a leading role, the letter should establish that the foreign national is (or was) a leader. A title, with appropriate matching duties, can help to establish if a role is (or was), in fact, leading. For a critical role, the letter should establish that the foreign national has contributed in a way that is of significant importance to the outcome of the organization or establishment's activities. A supporting role may be considered "critical" if the foreign national's performance in the role is (or was) important in that way. It is not the title of the foreign national's role, but rather the foreign national's performance in the role that determines whether the role is (or was) critical. It is important to document that the foreign national's role was leading or critical to the organization as a whole, not just a specific department.

Any independent objective evidence to document the leading or critical role of the foreign national should also be provided.

Commanding a High Salary/Remuneration Compared to Others in the Field

To meet this criterion it is necessary to demonstrate that the foreign national's salary or remuneration is high relative to others working in the field. The following evidence can be submitted in support thereof:

- Copies of the foreign national's W-2 or 1099 forms (or similar foreign tax documents that establish yearly wages earned outside the United States) for years in which the foreign national received a high salary in the field of endeavor.

- Media reports of notably high salaries earned by others in the foreign national's field.
- A list compiled by credible professional organization(s) of the top earners in a field.
- Geographical or position appropriate compensation surveys.
- Organization justifications to pay above the compensation data.
- Information from the United States Department of Labor or similar sources that show the salaries of others in the field as a basis to compare their salaries with the salary of the foreign national. If United States Department of Labor prevailing wage rate information is submitted, it must be accompanied by other corroborative evidence showing that the wage rate is high relative to others working in the field.
- Letters from other companies/organizations in the field discussing that the foreign national's salary is high relative to their employees who work in the field.

Commercial Success in the Performing Arts

This criterion is primarily for actors and recording artists. It focuses on the volume of sales and box office receipts as a measure of the foreign national's commercial success in the performing arts. Just because a foreign national has recorded and released musical compilations or performed in theatrical, motion picture, or television productions does not in and of itself meet this criterion. The evidence must show that the volume of sales and box office receipts reflect commercial success relative to others involved in similar pursuits in the performing arts.

This criterion should be documented by providing box office receipts or sales receipts for audio or video recordings to show success in the performing arts.

With regard to the catch-all category allowing for submission of other comparable evidence, an explanation must be provided as to why the ten enumerated regulatory criteria for which "comparable" evidence is being submitted are not applicable to the foreign national's occupation and why the evidence submitted is "comparable" to one of the ten enumerated regulatory criteria.

When preparing an EB-1A petition it is necessary to provide complete evidence in support of a specific category and to explain to USCIS exactly how the facts and evidence qualify the foreign national as meeting the legal requirements of a specific category. This should be done for each category for which evidence is provided regardless of whether it appears the legal requirements of a category are obviously met.

Part Two of the Extraordinary Ability Aliens Analysis

Pursuant to *Kazarian v. USCIS*,[2] if USCIS determines that the foreign national has received a one-time achievement award or has provided evidence to meet three of the ten enumerated regulatory requirements, USCIS undertakes a second step wherein the evidence is evaluated in its totality to determine whether the foreign national meets the overall requirements of the extraordinary ability aliens category of having received sustained national or international acclaim and having achievements that provide recognition as one of that small percentage who has risen to the very top of the field of endeavor.

The foreign national should persuade USCIS that the preponderance of the evidence demonstrates that the foreign national has the high level of expertise required for EB-1A approval. The author typically provides quotes from the experts regarding the foreign national's achievements, which indicate that the foreign national is one of the small percentage at the very top of the field. The author also summarizes the evidence to show that the evidence demonstrates that the foreign national has sustained national or international acclaim that has been maintained and has achievements that have been recognized in the field of expertise indicating that the foreign national is one of that small percentage who has risen to the very top of the field of endeavor. The "very top of the field" does not mean that the foreign national is at the top 1 percent of

---

[2] *Kazarian v. U.S. Citizenship & Immigration Servs.*, 596 F.3d 1115 (9th Cir. 2010).

the field as USCIS officers are trained to look for the top 15 percent or 20 percent of the field.

The EB-1A petition package submitted to USCIS should include Form I-140; Form G-28 if represented by an attorney (which is recommended); Form I-907 (if premium processing is utilized); check(s) for the filing fee and premium processing fee (if applicable); a detailed cover letter, evidence of plans for work in the United States, the foreign national's *curriculum vita;* the foreign national's academic qualifications; and documentary evidence that the foreign national meets the legal requirements for EB-1A approval.

The EB-1A extraordinary ability aliens category is an excellent category to apply for a green card for those who are among the small percentage at the very top of their field of endeavor. A green card can be obtained based on one's own accomplishments without regard to the availability of United States workers and without the need for employer sponsorship.

2

EB-1B Outstanding Professors and Researchers

A professor or researcher who shows that he or she is internationally recognized as outstanding in a specific academic field may qualify for a green card under the first preference employment-based category known as outstanding professors and researchers (EB-1B). EB-1B requires that the foreign national have a full-time permanent job offer in the United States in the academic field at a university (for professors or researchers) or a qualifying private employer (for researchers) and at least three years of teaching and/or research experience in the academic field. The petition to USCIS is filed by the prospective United States employer, not the foreign national. In other words, unlike the EB-1A extraordinary ability aliens and EB-2 national interest waiver categories, self-filing is not permitted in the EB-1B outstanding professors and researchers category.

Per the Code of Federal Regulations, academic field means a body of specialized knowledge offered for study at an accredited United States university or institution of higher education.

The sponsoring employer must provide a letter demonstrating an offer of full-time employment for a tenured or tenure-track teaching or a comparable permanent research position in the United States. Permanent, in reference to a research position, means either tenured, tenure-track, or for a term of indefinite or unlimited duration, and in which the employee will ordinarily have an expectation of continued employment unless there is good cause for termination.

If the position is a teaching position, it must be at a university or an institution of higher education. If the position is a research position, it may be at a university or institution of higher education or may be a comparable position with a private employer if that private employer meets certain additional requirements regarding research accomplishments and the number of researchers employed.

When filing an EB-1B petition, the sponsoring employer must provide evidence of its ability to pay the offered wage to the professor or researcher. Ability to pay the offered wage is demonstrated by providing copies of annual reports, federal tax returns, or audited financial statements. Net income or net current assets equal to or greater than the wage offered will establish ability to pay. If the employer is employing the foreign national and has paid or currently is paying the offered wage, it is evidence of ability to pay the offered wage. If the employer has one hundred or more employees, the employer may submit a statement from a financial officer of the employer that establishes the ability to pay the offered wage. The employer may also submit additional evidence such as profit/loss statements, bank account records, or personnel records where appropriate.

Credentials of the Foreign National

Eligibility in the EB-1B category requires that the foreign national have a minimum of three years of teaching and/or research experience in the academic field. Experience in teaching or research while working on an advanced degree will only be acceptable if the foreign national has acquired the degree, and if the teaching duties were such that he or she had full responsibility for the class(es) taught or if the research conducted toward the degree has been recognized within the academic field as outstanding. Evidence of teaching and/or research experience must be in the form of letter(s) from current or former employer(s) and must include the name, address, and title of the writer, and a specific description of the duties performed by the foreign national.

To demonstrate that the foreign national is internationally recognized as outstanding in the particular academic field, the EB-1B petition must be supported by documentation that the foreign national meets at least two of the following six criteria, similar to those in the EB-1A category:

- Documentation of the foreign national's receipt of major prizes or awards for outstanding achievement in the academic field;
- Documentation of the foreign national's membership in associations in the academic field which require outstanding achievements of their members;
- Published material in professional publications written by others about the foreign national's work in the academic field. Such material must include the title, date, and author of the material and any necessary translation;
- Evidence of the foreign national's participation, either individually or on a panel, as the judge of the work of others in the same or an allied academic field;
- Evidence of the foreign national's original scientific or scholarly research contributions to the academic field; or
- Evidence of the foreign national's authorship of scholarly books or articles (in scholarly journals with international circulation) in the academic field.

The nature of the evidence submitted in support of each EB-1B category is similar to the evidence submitted in support of the comparable EB-1A category discussed in Chapter 1 and those guidelines should be referenced when preparing evidence for an EB-1B petition. It should be noted, however, that there are subtle differences in the language of the EB-1B categories versus the comparable EB-1A categories. Specifically:

- EB-1B requires receipt of major prizes or awards for outstanding achievement in the academic field whereas EB-1A requires receipt of lesser nationally or internationally recognized prizes or awards for excellence in the field of endeavor.
- EB-1B requires membership in associations in the academic field that require outstanding achievements of their members whereas EB-1A has an additional requirement that membership be judged by recognized national or international experts in their disciplines or fields.
- EB-1B only references published material about the foreign national in professional publications whereas EB-1A references published material about the foreign national in professional publications, major trade publications, or other major media.

- EB-1B requires original scientific or scholarly research contributions to the academic field whereas EB-1A requires original scientific or scholarly contributions of major significance.
- EB-1B requires articles published by the foreign national in scholarly books or articles in scholarly journals with international circulation whereas EB-1A allows for articles published by the foreign national in professional or major trade publications or other major media.

Additionally, EB-1A has additional categories and a "catch-all" category that are not available for EB-1B.

These differences in evidentiary standards between the two categories must be taken into consideration both in deciding whether to file in the EB-1B or EB-1A category and in preparing the petition for submission to USCIS. The foreign national must demonstrate by a preponderance of the evidence that international recognition is outstanding.

Offer of Employment

Unlike aliens in the extraordinary ability category, aliens in the outstanding professors and researchers category must have a job offer. However, as with all first preference employment petitions, no PERM Labor Certification is required. USCIS regulations require that the offer of employment be in the form of a letter from:

- A United States university or institution of higher learning offering the foreign national a tenured or tenure-track teaching position in the foreign national's academic field;
- A United States university or institution of higher learning offering the foreign national a permanent research position in the foreign national's academic field; or
- A department, division, or institute of a private employer offering the foreign national a permanent research position in the foreign national's academic field. The department, division, or institute must demonstrate that it employs at least three persons full-time in research positions, and that it has achieved documented accomplishments in an academic field.

When preparing an EB-1B petition on behalf of a university, the author provides both an original letter from an authorized hiring official addressed to USCIS describing the offer of employment and a copy of a letter from an authorized hiring official addressed to the foreign national offering the foreign national the permanent teaching or research position. Set forth below are sample letters for a permanent research position:

Sample Letter to USCIS

> Dear Officer:
>
> _____ University is offering Dr. _____ a permanent full-time research position as a _____ at an annual salary of $_____.
>
> We would like Dr. _____ to work for our University in the academic field of Molecular Genetics where he will conduct research to determine the role genes play during liver regeneration in order to treat alcoholic liver diseases.
>
> Dr. _____ has the required three years of research experience in the academic field of Molecular Genetics as he has been employed by _____ University performing the above-referenced job duties since _____[date].
>
> The _____ position is funded through multi-year grants and _____ University intends to continue to seek additional multi-year grants for the position as such funding is normally renewed. There is a reasonable expectation that funding will continue beyond the existing grants as this is a long-term research project. As such, this offer is intended to be of an indefinite or unlimited duration and the nature of the position is such that Dr. _____ will ordinarily have an expectation of continued employment. Dr. _____'s employment is considered permanent within the meaning of 8 C.F.R. § 204.5(i)(2).

Thank you for your consideration.

Sincerely,

Sample Letter to Foreign National

Dear Dr. _____ :

_____ University is offering you a permanent research position as a _____ at an annual salary of $_____ that will change your existing employment status from that of temporary to permanent employment if you are granted United States Permanent Resident Status by the United States Citizenship and Immigration Services. As the _____[Title], I am authorized by _____ University to extend this offer of employment.

Although your employment is "at will," the offered position is a permanent position intended to be of indefinite or unlimited duration and the nature of the position is such that you will ordinarily have an expectation of continued employment. The position is covered by multi-year grants and funding for the position is expected to continue.

Sincerely,

If present and/or former grants and/or employment contracts are available such documentation can also evidence the permanent offer of employment.

The author would provide comparable letters if the sponsoring employer were a private employer. Additionally, for a private employer it is necessary to document that the private employer has a department, division, or institute that employs at least three persons full-time in research positions and has achieved documented accomplishments in an academic field. Evidence to demonstrate that the private employer has a department, division, or institute that employs at least three persons full-time in research positions can include lists of employees conducting research in the department, division, or institute with a discussion of their research, copies of the *curriculum vitae* of the employees, an overview of the employer, and payroll records of the employer evidencing actual employment of three or more researchers. The researchers must be engaged in full-time research in the foreign national's field, which is usually the case if all researchers are pursuing a common objective. Evidence to demonstrate that the private employer has a department, division, or institute that has achieved documented accomplishments in the field can include news articles, press releases, awards, publications, patents, grant funding, commercial success, etc., setting forth the accomplishments. The employer's annual report and/or mission statement, websites discussing the employer's accomplishments, and independent expert support letters about the employer's accomplishments can also be utilized as evidence.

An offer letter for a non-research professor would need to indicate the position is tenured or tenure-track.

Finally, just like in the EB-1A category, even if the above evidentiary criteria are met, pursuant to the federal court case *Kazarian v. USCIS*, USCIS will review the evidence as a whole to determine whether the foreign national meets the overall eligibility standard for the EB-1B category by a preponderance of the evidence.[3] For these reasons, it is always critical that the foreign national never take for granted that USCIS will understand that the evidence submitted meets the evidentiary standard for EB-1B. It is necessary to thoroughly present and explain all of the facts and evidence in a manner that relates the facts and evidence to the EB-1B legal requirements.

The advantage of EB-1B over EB-1A is that the evidentiary standard is lower for EB-1B, thereby making approval of EB-1B "easier" than EB-1A. It is also helpful to have the backing of a university or private employer as it eliminates any question that the foreign national will be working in the field of endeavor.

---

[3] *Kazarian v. U.S. Citizenship & Immigration Servs.*, 596 F.3d 1115 (9th Cir. 2010).

There are several disadvantages of EB-1B compared to EB-1A. First, EB-1B is not available to postdoctoral researchers as a postdoctoral position is not a permanent research position. An EB-1B must be for a permanent research position such as research associate, research fellow, and so on. Second, self-filing is not permitted, so the employer must agree to file the I-140 petition. In certain circumstances, an employer will require the use of a specific attorney who the foreign national does not wish to have prepare the case or who charges fees that are not agreeable to the foreign national but that the foreign national has no choice but to pay. The foreign national may choose his or her own attorney in a self-filed EB-1A case. Third, in an EB-1B petition, the foreign national does not have the same job flexibility as in an EB-1A petition. In an EB-1B petition the foreign national may change employers to work in a position that is "same or similar" to the position set forth in the I-140 petition only with an approved I-140 petition and an I-485 application that has been pending for more than 180 days. It should be noted that USCIS generally adjudicates I-485 applications in less than 180 days, eliminating the possibility to change jobs before green card approval. The foreign national is also limited as to when he or she may change employers after an EB-1B green card approval as there is an undefined amount of time a foreign national must work for a sponsoring employer upon receipt of a green card to avoid a finding of fraud, which could become an issue if the foreign national eventually applies for United States citizenship. In an EB-1A petition, the foreign national may change jobs in the same field without any effect on the green card.

The EB-1B petition package submitted to USCIS should include Form I-140; Form G-28 if represented by an attorney (which is recommended); Form I-907 (if premium processing is utilized); check(s) for the filing fee and premium processing fee (if applicable); a detailed cover letter; the foreign national's *curriculum vitae;* the foreign national's academic qualifications; the two job offer letters as referenced above along with any other evidence of the permanent offer of employment; evidence establishing that the foreign national has at least three years of experience in teaching and/or research in the academic field; proof of the employer's ability to pay the offered wage; for a research position with a private employer evidence of a department, division or institute of the private employer with at least three persons employed in full-time research positions and with documented accomplishments in the field, and documentary evidence that the foreign national meets the legal requirements for EB-1B approval.

Just like the EB-1A category, the EB-1B category is almost exclusively used by foreign nationals chargeable to India or China, as foreign nationals from the rest of the world would generally choose to self-file a national interest waiver petition that has a lower evidentiary standard than EB-1B and has no backlog to file for a green card.

3

EB-2 National Interest Waiver

Under most circumstances, even foreign nationals who possess an advanced degree (i.e., a master's degree or higher), or exceptional ability in the sciences, arts, or business, are only eligible for a green card in the EB-2 category by undergoing the PERM Labor Certification process with an employer sponsor. However, if a foreign national qualifies for a national interest waiver, a foreign national may self-petition for a green card. A national interest waiver petition allows a foreign national to obtain a waiver of the job offer requirement and avoid the PERM Labor Certification process altogether, which can be lengthy and expensive and could ultimately be denied in the event of a United States worker being available for the offered position. While the national interest waiver allows a foreign national to self-petition, an employer may file a national interest waiver petition on behalf of a foreign national, although this is almost never done in practice. A foreign national changing employment does not affect the validity of a national interest waiver petition so long as the foreign national continues to work in the field that was the basis for the national interest waiver.

To obtain a green card through a national interest waiver, a foreign national must establish a past record that justifies projections of future benefits to the national interest of the United States. Eligibility for a national interest waiver petition is set forth in the Administrative Appeals Office (AAO) Decision *Matter of New York State v. Department of Transportation* (NYSDOT), which standardized a three-part test to determine whether a foreign national is eligible for a national interest waiver. The foreign national must satisfy all three parts of the NYSDOT test and it is at the discretion of USCIS to grant a national interest waiver petition.[4]

---

[4] 22 I&N Dec. 215 (Comm. 1998).

Foreign nationals who are not from China or India and can meet the three-part NYSDOT test almost always file for a national interest waiver petition rather than an extraordinary ability aliens petition because the standard for approval for a national interest waiver petition is lower than for an extraordinary ability aliens petition. Additionally, there is typically no wait to file for a green card for a non-Chinese/Indian foreign national with an approved EB-2 national interest waiver petition. This is especially the case for scientific researchers with the qualifications to meet the three-part NYSDOT test. There may be certain instances where a foreign national not from China or India would qualify as an extraordinary ability alien but not for a national interest waiver petition, but those instances are rare. An additional difference between the two categories is that unlike an extraordinary ability aliens petition, a national interest waiver petition is not eligible for premium processing, but that should not be a reason for a non-Chinese/Indian foreign national to choose the extraordinary ability aliens category over the national interest waiver category.

The first part of the NYSDOT test is whether the foreign national seeks to work in an area of "substantial intrinsic merit," which seems to relate to the seven non-exclusive factors the AAO identified in the NYSDOT case as related to the general welfare: (1) improving the US economy, (2) improving wages and working conditions of US workers, (3) improving education and training programs for US children and underqualified workers, (4) improving health care, (5) providing more affordable housing for young and/or older, poorer US residents, (6) improving the US environment and making more productive use of natural resources, or (7) involving a request from an interested US government agency.

Most national interest waiver petitions, especially those for scientific researchers, involve work by the foreign national that is improving the US economy, improving health care, and/or improving the US environment and making more productive use of natural resources. However, not every engineer, scientist, businessperson, and so on, by virtue of his or her profession, automatically satisfies the first part of the NYSDOT test. Instead, USCIS takes a "case-by-case" approach in evaluating the intrinsic merit of a foreign worker's profession. It is important to explain to USCIS exactly how the foreign national is seeking work in an area that is of intrinsic merit.

Here is an example as to how the author explained to USCIS the substantial intrinsic merit of the work of a scientist whose field of research was biomarker discovery.

Sample Explanation for Part 1 of the NYSDOT National Interest Waiver Test

> Dr. XXX meets the first part of the NYSDOT test as his work is improving health care in the United States. Dr. XXX is conducting research to discover and analyze biomarkers that can be used to help diagnose/treat disease.
>
> A biomarker, or biological marker, is in general a substance used as an indicator of a biological state. It is a characteristic that is objectively measured and evaluated as an indicator of normal biological processes, pathogenic processes, or pharmacologic responses to a therapeutic intervention. A "biomarker" is a surrogate "marker" of disease. For example, "cholesterol" is a blood-based biomarker to assess the risk of heart disease. Biomarkers may help diagnose disease as well as monitor disease progression and response to treatment. The best biomarkers are accurate and simple and inexpensive to measure.
>
> Biomarker discovery is a scientific term describing the process by which biomarkers are discovered. Many commonly used blood tests in medicine are tests for biomarkers. There is interest in biomarker discovery on the part of the pharmaceutical industry as blood tests or other biomarker tests could serve as intermediate markers of disease in clinical trials, and as possible drug targets. An example of biomarker discovery is the use of insulin to assess kidney function. From this process, a naturally occurring molecule (creatinine) was discovered, enabling the same measurements to be made without insulin injections.
>
> The identification of clinically significant biomarkers of phenotype and biological function is an expanding area

of research that will extend diagnostic capabilities and therefore improve health care. Biomarkers for a number of diseases have recently emerged, including prostate specific antigen (PSA) for prostate cancer and C-reactive protein (CRP) for heart disease. Dr. XXX's research has identified biomarkers that can be used in the diagnosis of cancer and to overcome antibiotic resistance. Dr. XXX, for example, has discovered a biomarker for colon cancer that is present in stool and can be an alternative to the highly invasive colonoscopy procedure. Using biomarkers from easily assessable biofluids (e.g., blood, stool, and urine) is beneficial in evaluating the state of harder-to-reach tissues and organs. Biofluids are more readily accessible, unlike more invasive or unfeasible techniques (such as tissue biopsy).

The first and most important step of biomarker discovery and analysis is to plan a proteomic strategy. Each strategy needs to be custom-designed to achieve specific goals for each individual biomarker discovery project. The selection of the clinical samples is the second crucial step. It is necessary to select samples that are likely to contain biomarkers that can be identified using available resources. Mass spectrometry data must then be collected and a statistical analysis performed to rank the best matches. The final step of biomarker discovery and analysis is verification. Generally, this is an ELISA-based experiment performed with a different and larger sample set. Biomarker discovery and analysis requires extensive technical skill and knowledge and Dr. XXX is one of the top researchers in the world in this field.

The biomarkers discovered and analyzed by Dr. XXX have direct clinical implications in the diagnosis/treatment of cancer and resistance to antibiotics. As such, Dr. XXX's work is of great importance to health care in the United States. Dr. XXX is seeking to work in an area of substantial intrinsic merit as his research has far-reaching implications since the biomarkers he has discovered and analyzed benefit society by leading to better disease diagnosis and treatment.

The second part of the NYSDOT test is whether the benefit of the foreign national's proposed activity will be "national in scope." Essentially, the effect of the foreign national's work product cannot be local—the work must have a national impact. In the NYSDOT case, it was determined that a bridge engineer who worked on maintaining bridges and roads in New York performed work that was national in scope because New York's bridges and roads connect the state to the national transportation system and therefore proper maintenance of such bridges and roads serve the interests of other areas of the United States.

The work of researchers generally affects the health of individuals throughout the United States. Pursuits such as medical research are presumed to have a geographically distributed beneficial effect that will affect society by providing new medical treatment options. Work that is not health-care related can, for example, be shown to lead to a safer environment and the development of products used for commercial purposes by individuals in all fifty states. It is generally easier to prove the national scope of the work of scientists, doctors, and other researchers than business people, as the latter may seem more local or provincial. However, it is by no means impossible for those in business to obtain a national interest waiver; they have been granted for business people, especially in the case of someone who substantially improves their industry as a whole.

The third part of the NYSDOT test is whether the foreign national will serve the national interest to a substantially greater degree than would an available United States worker having the same minimum qualifications so that the avoidance of the PERM Labor Certification process (designed to locate any minimally qualified United States worker and intending to protect job opportunities of United States workers) is justified. To satisfy this third part of the NYSDOT test, the foreign national must demonstrate a "track record of success" "with some degree of influence on the field as a whole" above and beyond the substantial majority of others in the field. It is necessary to explain the importance of the work of the foreign national and its widespread impact at the national level, showing that contributions from the continued employment of the foreign national in the United States will significantly outweigh peers. In other words, it is necessary to provide documentation establishing the foreign national's accomplishments (including evidence from unbiased proponents and concrete documentation of past success), how the foreign national's accomplishments have had a degree of influence on the field as a whole, and how the foreign national's accomplishments have been more meaningful than the accomplishments of others in the field.

To qualify for a national interest waiver the foreign national's value must be so substantially greater than the value of a United States worker, that it would actually be contrary to the national interest to require the foreign national to go through the PERM Labor Certification process. This question of the benefits of the foreign worker outweighing the protections afforded by the PERM Labor Certification process runs throughout the other two prongs as well—a profession of little merit and/or of limited national scope could not benefit the United States enough to justify disregarding the interests of United States workers. Being important to a certain study or endeavor will not suffice; the foreign national must offer a substantially greater benefit than an American counterpart.

Fortunately, to obtain approval in the national interest waiver category a foreign national does not have to meet the "extraordinary ability" standard of the EB-1A extraordinary ability aliens category, which requires proof that the foreign national is in the very top tier of the field. Instead, the foreign national need only demonstrate noteworthy achievement relative to the substantial majority of others in the field.

Most national interest waiver petitions are filed by foreign nationals with an advanced degree. To show that the foreign national is a professional holding an advanced degree, the petition must be accompanied by:

- An official academic record showing that the foreign national has an advanced US degree or a foreign equivalent degree; or

- An official academic record showing that the foreign national has a US baccalaureate degree or a foreign equivalent degree, and evidence in the form of letters from current or former employer(s) showing that the foreign national has at least five years of progressive post-baccalaureate experience in the specialty

For those who have obtained an advanced degree, the following types of documentation, analogous to the evidence for the EB-1A extraordinary ability aliens category and EB-1B outstanding professors and researchers category, can be used to establish a record of success in the field: reference letters from industry leaders, officials of government agencies, professional trade associations, and independent experts; publications, patents, awards, prior speaking engagements, and conference presentations; judging the work of others in the field; discussion of the foreign national's work by others and in the media; citations; implementation of the foreign national's work by others; and memberships in associations that require achievement, etc. Keeping in mind the discretionary nature of the national interest waiver, in addition to letters from supervisors, it is generally advisable to secure recommendations, commendations, or evaluations from those who do not know the foreign national personally, as endorsements from independent parties are more persuasive.

Unlike in the EB-1A extraordinary ability aliens category and EB-1B outstanding professors and researchers category, there is no regulatory list of specific evidence that must be provided to obtain approval in the national interest waiver category, so the foreign national and his or her attorney should brainstorm as to the type of evidence that can be obtained to support that the foreign national meets the three-part NYSDOT test.

For those individuals who do not have an advanced degree, but have "exceptional ability" in the sciences, arts, or business, the PERM Labor Certification and job offer requirement may also be avoided through the national interest waiver exemption. Exceptional ability in the sciences, arts, or business means a degree of expertise significantly above that ordinarily encountered in the sciences, arts, or business. To qualify as having exceptional ability in the sciences, arts, or business, a foreign national must establish three factors from the following list, which are less stringent than the factors required for "extraordinary ability":

- An official academic record showing that the foreign national has a degree, diploma, certificate, or similar award from a college, university, school, or other institution of learning relating to the area of exceptional ability;
- Evidence in the form of letter(s) from current or former employer(s) showing that the foreign national has at least ten years of full-time experience in the occupation for which he or she is being sought;
- A license to practice the profession or certification for a particular profession or occupation;
- Evidence that the foreign national has commanded a salary, or other remuneration for services, that demonstrates exceptional ability;
- Evidence of membership in professional associations; or
- Evidence of recognition for achievements and significant contributions to the industry or field by peers, governmental entities, or professional or business organizations.

If the above standards do not readily apply to the foreign national's occupation, the foreign national may submit comparable evidence to establish eligibility.

The EB-2 national interest waiver petition package submitted to USCIS should include Form I-140; Form ETA 750B (in duplicate); Form G-28 if represented by an attorney (which is recommended); a check for the filing fee; a detailed cover letter; the foreign national's *curriculum vitae*; evidence of the foreign national's advanced degree or evidence that the foreign national meets the standard for classification as having exceptional ability in the sciences, arts, or business; and documentary evidence that the foreign national meets the legal requirements for national interest waiver approval.

4

EB-2 National Interest Waiver for Entrepreneurs

USCIS has taken measures to increase the number of foreign entrepreneurs in the United States to further economic development. The agency indicated that a national interest waiver petition is available to entrepreneurs. This obviates the need for a qualifying job offer and PERM Labor Certification for qualified entrepreneurs and allows an entrepreneur to self-file a national interest waiver petition.

Entrepreneurs still must be professionals holding an advanced degree or have exceptional ability and still must meet the three-part *Matter of New York State v. Department of Transportation* (NYSDOT) test.[5]

Under the first part of the NYSDOT test, the entrepreneur must seek employment in an area that has substantial intrinsic merit. To meet this test, a foreign national should focus on how the entrepreneurial venture brings economic value to the United States. The foreign national should indicate to USCIS exactly how the business will benefit the economy of the United States (as well as any other areas such as health care, the environment, etc.). Evidence of the introduction of new goods and/or services into the marketplace, new income streams, job creation, and so on, should be provided to establish the substantial intrinsic merit of the entrepreneur's business.

The second part of the NYSDOT test requires that the entrepreneur demonstrate that the proposed benefit to be provided will be national in

---

[5] *See* 22 I&N Dec. 215 (Comm. 1998).

scope. To meet this test the entrepreneur can show that jobs created by the business venture on a local level will also create (or spin off) related jobs in other parts of the United States or that jobs created locally will have a positive national impact. The focus should be on job creation and the economic effects of such employment. Local jobs can have a national impact in a variety of ways, such as goods/services being distributed on a national level, employees contributing to the economy on a national level, and jobs in one location leading to new jobs in another location. A combination of factors can be used to show that the fruits of a business venture are beneficial on a national level.

The third part of the NYSDOT test requires that the foreign entrepreneur seeking an exemption from the PERM Labor Certification process present a national benefit so great as to outweigh the national interest inherent in the PERM Labor Certification process designed to protect the jobs of United States workers. The foreign entrepreneur must "present a significant benefit to the field of endeavor." The field must be the same as that identified in part one of the three-part test and the entrepreneur must document how the entrepreneurial enterprise will benefit that field.

NYSDOT states:

> In all cases, while the national interest waiver hinges on prospective national benefit, it clearly must be established that the beneficiary's past record justifies projections of future benefit to the national interest. The petitioner's subjective assurance that the beneficiary will, in the future, serve the national interest cannot suffice to establish prospective national benefit if the beneficiary has few or no demonstrable achievements.

The entrepreneur who demonstrates that the business enterprise will create jobs for United States workers or otherwise enhance the welfare of the United States may qualify for a national interest waiver petition. For example, the entrepreneur may not be taking a job opportunity from a United States worker but instead may be creating new job opportunities for them. The creation of jobs domestically for United States workers may serve the national interest to a substantially greater degree than the work of others in the same field.

The focus of an entrepreneurial national interest waiver petition is clearly on job creation. It is critical that the third part of the NYSDOT test prove that the national interest would not be as well served by allowing a United States worker with the same minimum qualifications to "run the business" of the foreign entrepreneur instead of the foreign entrepreneur. Evidence of concrete past achievement must indicate the ability of the foreign entrepreneur to serve the national interest in justification of the projection of future benefits to the United States economy and any other applicable area. The evidence must be able to show that requiring a PERM Labor Certification for the foreign entrepreneur would adversely affect the national interest of boosting the United States economy and creating jobs.

As with a standard national interest waiver petition, there are no defined categories of evidence that must be submitted with an entrepreneur national interest waiver petition. The type of evidence that can be submitted includes but is not limited to evidence of prior successful business ventures, business plans for prior successful ventures to show that the foreign entrepreneur's prior businesses met their objectives, current number of employees, business awards, major contracts or deals, media coverage, and a detailed business plan for the entrepreneur's business including income and job creation projections. The past accomplishments of the foreign national as an entrepreneur should be emphasized to justify the projection that the proposed business enterprise in the United States will benefit the United States economy and create jobs. The key is to demonstrate that the foreign national applying for a national interest waiver petition as an entrepreneur has a "track record of success" as an entrepreneur. The projection of future benefits to the US economy on a national level must be supported by concrete documentation of the foreign national's past achievements as an entrepreneur.

5

O-1 Nonimmigrant Visa for Extraordinary Ability Workers

The O-1 visa is a temporary work visa available to those foreign nationals who have "extraordinary ability in the sciences, arts, education, business or athletics" that "has been demonstrated by sustained national or international acclaim." USCIS interprets the statute very broadly to encompass most fields of creative endeavor. For example, chefs, carpenters, and lecturers can all obtain O-1 visas. The foreign national entering the United States must be coming to work in his or her field of ability, but the position need not require the services of a person of extraordinary ability. The O-1 visa is an attractive option for qualified foreign nationals who may not be eligible for H-1B status such as in a situation where they are subject to the two-year J-1 home residency requirement, or are unable to receive an H-1B cap number, or have reached their six-year maximum stay in H-1B status. It is also an attractive option for qualified foreign nationals who do not wish to permanently reside in the United States but only seek to work in the United States for a temporary period. An O-1 visa requires employer sponsorship.

O-1A visas cover foreign nationals who have extraordinary ability in the sciences, arts, education, business, or athletics, while O-1B visas are specifically available to foreign nationals who have demonstrated a record of extraordinary achievement in motion picture or TV production. To obtain an O-1A or O-1B visa, the foreign national's employer must file a Form I-129 petition for a nonimmigrant worker on the foreign national's behalf. This petition must demonstrate, through affidavits by employers and experts, contracts, awards, advisory opinions, and other documentary evidence, that the foreign national possesses a level of skill or achievement in his or her field that is of national or international repute. The regulations state that the foreign national either must show the receipt of an internationally recognized award (i.e. Nobel Prize), or be able to satisfy three out of eight criteria listed to establish such acclaim. These criteria are generally the same for O-1A and O-1B visa holders, although the latter are held to a higher standard.

The standard for an O-1 visa is substantially similar to the EB-1A extraordinary ability aliens category. To obtain an O-1 visa, foreign nationals must demonstrate that they possess "a level of expertise indicating that the person is one of the small percentage who have risen to the top of the field of endeavor." Absent a major internationally recognized award, such expertise is demonstrated by providing documentation in three of the following categories:

Evidentiary Criteria for an O-1 Foreign National of Extraordinary Ability in the Fields of Science, Education, Business, or Athletics

A foreign national of extraordinary ability in the fields of science, education, business, or athletics must demonstrate sustained national or international acclaim and recognition for achievements in the field of expertise by providing evidence of receipt of a major, internationally recognized award, such as the Nobel Prize or at least three of the following forms of documentation:

- Documentation of the foreign national's receipt of nationally or internationally recognized prizes or awards for excellence in the field of endeavor;
- Documentation of the foreign national's membership in associations in the field for which classification is sought, which require outstanding achievements of their members, as judged by recognized national or international experts in their disciplines or fields;
- Published material in professional or major trade publications or major media about the foreign national, relating to the foreign national's work in the field for which classification is sought,

which shall include the title, date, and author of such published material, and any necessary translation;

- Evidence of the foreign national's participation on a panel, or individually, as a judge of the work of others in the same or in an allied field of specialization to that for which classification is sought;
- Evidence of the foreign national's original scientific, scholarly, or business-related contributions of major significance in the field;
- Evidence of the foreign national's authorship of scholarly articles in the field, in professional journals, or other major media;
- Evidence that the foreign national has been employed in a critical or essential capacity for organizations and establishments that have a distinguished reputation;
- Evidence that the foreign national has either commanded a high salary or will command a high salary or other remuneration for services, evidenced by contracts or other reliable evidence.

Comparable evidence may be submitted if any of the above categories do not readily apply.

Evidentiary Criteria for an O-1 Foreign National of Extraordinary Ability in the Arts

To qualify as a foreign national of extraordinary ability in the field of arts, the foreign national must be recognized as being prominent in his or her field of endeavor as demonstrated by the following:

Evidence that the foreign national has been nominated for, or has been the recipient of, significant national or international awards or prizes in the particular field such as an Academy Award, an Emmy, a Grammy, or a Director's Guild Award or at least three of the following forms of documentation:

- Evidence that the foreign national has performed, and will perform, services as a lead or starring participant in productions or events that have a distinguished reputation as evidenced by critical reviews, advertisements, publicity releases, publications contracts, or endorsements;

- Evidence that the foreign national has achieved national or international recognition for achievements evidenced by critical reviews or other published materials by or about the individual in major newspapers, trade journals, magazines, or other publications;
- Evidence that the foreign national has performed, and will perform, in a lead, starring, or critical role for organizations and establishments that have a distinguished reputation evidenced by articles in newspapers, trade journals, publications, or testimonials;
- Evidence that the foreign national has a record of major commercial or critically acclaimed successes as evidenced by such indicators as title, rating, standing in the field, box office receipts, motion pictures or television ratings, and other occupational achievements reported in trade journals, major newspapers, or other publications;
- Evidence that the foreign national has received significant recognition for achievements from organizations, critics, government agencies, or other recognized experts in the field in which the foreign national is engaged. Such testimonials must be in a form that clearly indicates the author's authority, expertise, and knowledge of the foreign national's achievements;
- Evidence that the foreign national has either commanded a high salary or will command a high salary or other substantial remuneration for services in relation to others in the field, as evidenced by contracts or other reliable evidence.

Comparable evidence may be submitted if any of the above categories do not readily apply.

Evidentiary Criteria for a Foreign National of Extraordinary Achievement in the Motion Picture or Television Industry

To qualify as a foreign national of extraordinary achievement in the motion picture or television industry, the foreign national must be recognized as having a demonstrated record of extraordinary achievement as evidenced by the following:

Evidence that the foreign national has been nominated for, or has been the recipient of, significant national or international awards or prizes in the particular field such as an Academy Award, an Emmy, a Grammy, or a Director's Guild Award or at least three of the following forms of documentation:

- Evidence that the foreign national has performed, and will perform, services as a lead or starring participant in productions or events which have a distinguished reputation as evidenced by critical reviews, advertisements, publicity releases, publications contracts, or endorsements;
- Evidence that the foreign national has achieved national or international recognition for achievements evidenced by critical reviews or other published materials by or about the foreign national in major newspapers, trade journals, magazines, or other publications;
- Evidence that the foreign national has performed, and will perform, in a lead, starring, or critical role for organizations and establishments that have a distinguished reputation evidenced by articles in newspapers, trade journals, publications, or testimonials;
- Evidence that the foreign national has a record of major commercial or critically acclaimed successes as evidenced by such indicators as title, rating, standing in the field, box office receipts, motion picture or television ratings, and other occupational achievements reported in trade journals, major newspapers, or other publications;
- Evidence that the foreign national has received significant recognition for achievements from organizations, critics, government agencies, or other recognized experts in the field in which the foreign national is engaged. Such testimonials must be in a form which clearly indicates the author's authority, expertise, and knowledge of the foreign national's achievements; Evidence that the foreign national has either commanded a high salary or will command a high salary or other substantial remuneration for services in relation to others in the field, as evidenced by contracts or other reliable evidence.

As mentioned above, the O-1 visa does not mandate that the petitioning employer require an employee of extraordinary ability to fill the position the foreign national seeks. Rather, the petitioning employer must show that the foreign national's abilities, skill, or achievements place the foreign national in the upper echelon of his or her profession and that the foreign national will continue to work in his or her field while in the United States. The number of available O-1 visas is unlimited. If granted, the O-1 visa can last up to three years initially, and may be extended in one-year increments. Lastly, if the O-1 visa holder changes employers, the new employer will have to file a Form I-129 petition and that petition must be approved before the foreign national may begin working for the new employer. Premium processing is available for O-1 status and is generally used in a change of employer situation.

The O-2 visa covers foreign nationals who seek temporary admission to the United States to accompany or assist the O-1 visa holder in the performance of a specific event or series of events. Examples of such events are scientific projects, conferences, lectures, conventions, exhibits, business projects, academic years, or engagements. A series of such events constitutes a single event for the purposes of applying for an O-2 visa. To establish eligibility for an O-2 visa, the petitioning employer must file a separate petition that demonstrates that the foreign national for whom it seeks the O-2 visa: (1) is an integral part of the actual performance; (2) has critical skills and experience with the O-1 visa holder, which are of a general nature and could not be performed by anyone; and (3) that the foreign national has nonimmigrant intent, which means the foreign national has a home in his or her country of residence that he or she does not intend to abandon. As O-2 visa holder's permission to be and work in the United States is contingent upon providing services to the O-1 visa holder and an O-2 visa holder may not change employers unless his or her O-1 visa holder changes employers.

O-3 visas are available to the spouses and children of O-1 and O-2 visa holders that are accompanying them or following to join them. The definitions of spouse and children are the same as in other immigration contexts.

Before a foreign national will be granted an O-1 visa, USCIS requires a consultation with a US-based organization. The petition must include a written advisory opinion from a peer group, labor union, or person(s) with expertise in the foreign national's field. Consultations are advisory and are not binding on USCIS but in almost every case a favorable advisory opinion can be obtained. If the advisory opinion is favorable to the petitioning employer, it should describe the foreign national's ability and achievements in the field of endeavor, describe the nature of the duties to be performed, and state whether the position requires the services of an alien of extraordinary ability. A consulting organization may also submit a letter of no objection in lieu of the above if it has no objection to the approval of the petition.

Set forth below is a sample outline of an advisory opinion letter used in the case of an O-1A researcher with extraordinary ability in science in the field of microbiology/ biotechnology.

Sample Outline of O-1A Advisory Opinion Letter

> Please accept this letter in satisfaction of the Consultation requirements for an O-1 Alien of Extraordinary Ability Petition in accordance with 8 C.F.R. 214. 2(o)(3)(ii) as I am a person with expertise in the field of microbiology/ biotechnology. I have no objection to and support the I-129 Petition for Nonimmigrant Worker being filed by University of _____ with United States Citizenship and Immigration Services to classify Dr. _____ as an O-1 Alien of Extraordinary Ability in the field of microbiology/biotechnology related to bacteria including botulinum neurotoxin. There is no labor union for the position and therefore I am acting as a consulting expert in the field.
>
> [Author Provides Background Information]
>
> I am well qualified to assess the research work, contribution and credentials of Dr. _____. I have not collaborated or worked with Dr. _____, but am

familiar with his research findings through his publications and conference presentations and through News Reports.

Dr. _____ is seeking a position at University of _____ as a Research Associate where he will conduct research on the botulinum neurotoxin for biodefense and medicinal purposes to minimize its threat as a weapon and to treat neurological disorders. The duties of his position involve carrying out bench work for the following set of experiments: growing cell culture; isolating proteins and nucleic acids; analyzing the effect of botulinum toxins on cells in terms of metabolic changes, gene expression and immune response; preparing reports to be submitted to funding agencies; making presentations to inside and outside researchers; planning and executing research; assisting in developing ideas for funding; and participating in strategic research planning of the University of _____.

[Discussion of the Foreign National's Ability and Achievements in the Field of Endeavor]

To summarize, Dr. _____ is a leading expert in microbiology/biotechnology related to bacteria and his discoveries with regard to botulinum neurotoxin have tremendous significance in terms of biotechnological and biomedical applications. He is a multidisciplinary expert and his discoveries made significant advancements in the fundamental understanding of bacterial gene regulation in response to abiotic stress factors. His outstanding publications that have been frequently discussed by others, receipt of many highly competitive awards/fellowships at the national and international level, membership in associations, and peer-review activity judging the work of others certainly classify Dr. _____ as an individual with extraordinary achievements. He has received sustained international acclaim for his findings and is unquestionably one of the small percentage of researchers who has risen to the very top of the field.

The Research Associate position offered to Dr. _____ requires a highly demanding technology background, interdisciplinary knowledge, and experience in handling complicated toxin samples, with immense BioSafety Level-3 (BSL-3) training under bio-containment conditions along with Security Risk Assessment (SRA approval) by the Federal Bureau of Investigation (FBI), Criminal Justice Information Services Division (CJIS).

As evidenced by his background and achievements discussed above, Dr. _____ is fully qualified for the Research Associate position. His extraordinary abilities with multidisciplinary experience are unique and rare. Such expertise is needed in the interests of National Biosecurity, since there is a continuing paucity of researchers conducting basic, clinical, and translational research on Priority Pathogens and biothreat toxins like Botulinum Neurotoxins, to discover methods to prevent and treat these agents. There are in fact several career development programs in the United States intended to increase the pool of highly skilled investigators in all aspects of research on Priority Pathogens, by integrating educational and training efforts from both basic science and clinical aspects, but there remains a shortage.

Dr. _____ has my strongest recommendation for his O-1 visa petition based on his extraordinary ability. Please do not hesitate to contact me for any further consultation.

Sincerely,

The form for petitioning for the O-1 visa is the I-129. This must be submitted along with the consultation opinion, evidence documenting the foreign national's extraordinary ability, and details of the proposed work in the United States. The petition is to be approved for the duration of the event in which the foreign national will participate, for a maximum of three years.

An O-1 visa may be extended in one-year increments for an indefinite period. Form I-129 is also used to file for an extension.

Finally, O-1 visas are what are known as "dual intent visas," meaning that even if the foreign national has filed for permanent resident status based on a PERM Labor Certification or petition for classification as a preference worker, the O visa cannot be denied. A foreign national granted an O-1 visa is in a good position to qualify in the EB-1A extraordinary ability aliens category but holding O-1 status does not guarantee approval of an EB-1A immigrant visa petition. "Extraordinary" for O-1 visa purposes does not necessarily equate to "extraordinary" for obtaining permanent resident status.

6

P Nonimmigrant Visa for Athletes, Artists, and Entertainers

The P-1, P-2, and P-3 visas are for foreign nationals who will be coming to the United States to perform as athletes, artists, or entertainers who do not meet the extraordinary ability alien requirements of an O-1 visa.

P-1 Visas

P-1 visas are for a foreign national who is a member of an entertainment group with an international reputation that is coming to the United States to perform or is an athlete with international recognition or who is part of a team with international recognition coming to the United States to compete individually or as part of a team in a specific athletic competition.

P-1 visas are generally utilized by entertainers and athletes who perform as part of an entertainment group or team for a specific event(s) such as a concert tour or a sports season. Work authorization is limited to employment for the entertainment group or team.

P-1 visas may be granted to each member of an entertainment group or team based on the international reputation of the entertainment group or team as a whole or may be granted to an individual based on the individual's international reputation.

A P-1 visa petition must include a written contract between the foreign national and the petitioning employer or an explanation of the oral agreement in the absence of a written agreement, an explanation of the nature of the performance(s)/competition(s), an itinerary, and a consultation from a labor organization similar to the O-1 category.

P-1 Entertainers

Dance and acting companies, circuses, choirs, orchestras, and pop/rock bands can utilize the P-1 category for their members to obtain a visa to come to the United States to perform. The P-1 visa is limited to foreign nationals who are members of an entertainment group. Individual performers are ineligible for a P-1 visa unless coming to the United States to join a foreign entertainment group already performing in the United States.

The P-1 entertainment group must have been internationally recognized as outstanding for a sustained and substantial period of time but if the entertainment group is only nationally recognized that could be sufficient if the entertainment group had difficulty demonstrating recognition in more than one country due to such factors as limited access to news media or consequences of geography. The entertainment group also must have been established for at least a period of one year.

To be eligible for a P-1 visa as a member of an entertainment group, an individual must have been with that group for a period of at least one year with certain exceptions. For example, this requirement only applies to 75 percent of the group's members, does not apply to a foreign national replacing an essential member of the group in the case of illness or unanticipated and exigent circumstances, and does not apply when the foreign national enhances the group in a critical role. The one-year requirement is also not imposed on circus personnel if the circus is nationally recognized.

A petition for P-1 classification for the members of an entertainment group shall be accompanied by:

- Evidence that the group has been established and performing regularly for a period of at least one year;
- A statement from the petitioner listing each member of the group and the exact dates for which each member has been employed on a regular basis by the group; and

- Evidence that the group has been internationally recognized in the discipline for a sustained and substantial period. This may be demonstrated by the submission of evidence of the group's nomination or receipt of significant international awards or prizes for outstanding achievement in its field or by three of the following different types of documentation:

  o Evidence that the group has performed, and will perform, as a starring or leading entertainment group in productions or events that have a distinguished reputation as evidenced by critical reviews, advertisements, publicity releases, publications, contracts, or endorsements;

  o Evidence that the group has achieved international recognition and acclaim for outstanding achievement in its field as evidenced by reviews in major newspapers, trade journals, magazines, or other published material;

  o Evidence that the group has performed, and will perform, services as a leading or starring group for organizations and establishments that have a distinguished reputation evidenced by articles in newspapers, trade journals, publications, or testimonials;

  o Evidence that the group has a record of major commercial or critically acclaimed successes, as evidenced by such indicators as ratings; standing in the field; box office receipts; record, cassette, or video sales; and other achievements in the field as reported in trade journals, major newspapers, or other publications;

  o Evidence that the group has achieved significant recognition for achievements from organizations, critics, government agencies, or other recognized experts in the field. Such testimonials must be in a form that clearly indicates the author's authority, expertise, and knowledge of the alien's achievements; or

  o Evidence that the group has commanded a high salary or will command a high salary or other substantial remuneration for services comparable to others similarly situated in the field as evidenced by contracts or other reliable evidence.

P-1 Athletes

The P-1 visa can be utilized by athletes in myriad different sports. It encompasses athletes who compete individually, in certain professional leagues and their minor league affiliates, certain amateur leagues (coaches can also qualify), and athletes in ice skating productions.

A P-1 athlete must be coming to the United States to participate in an athletic competition that has a distinguished reputation where athletes or athletic teams with an international reputation participate.

An individual athlete with an international reputation or who is a member of a foreign team that is internationally recognized qualifies for a P-1 visa. The foreign national must be coming to the United States to participate in an athletic competition with a distinguished reputation that requires participation of an athlete or a foreign athletic team with an international reputation.

Most athletes who play for major and minor league sports leagues are in the United States in P-1 status. There are no limitations on the number of P-1 athletes per team or the total number of P-1 athletes in the United States. An athlete who is traded retains legal status so long as the new team files a change of team petition with USCIS within thirty days of the trade.

A petition for an athletic team must be accompanied by evidence that the team as a unit has achieved international recognition in the sport. Each member of the team is accorded P-1 classification based on the international reputation of the team. A petition for an athlete who will compete individually or as a member of a United States team must be accompanied by evidence that the athlete has achieved international recognition in the sport based on his or her reputation.

A petition for a P-1 athlete or athletic team shall include:

- A tendered contract with a major United States sports league or team, or a tendered contract in an individual sport commensurate with international recognition in that sport, if such contracts are normally executed in the sport, and

- Documentation of at least two of the following:

  o Evidence of having participated to a significant extent in a prior season with a major United States sports league;
  o Evidence of having participated in international competition with a national team;
  o Evidence of having participated to a significant extent in a prior season for a United States college or university in intercollegiate competition;
  o A written statement from an official of the governing body of the sport which details how the foreign national or team is internationally recognized;
  o A written statement from a member of the sports media or a recognized expert in the sport which details how the foreign national or team is internationally recognized;
  o Evidence that the individual or team is ranked if the sport has international rankings; or
  o Evidence that the foreign national or team has received a significant honor or award in the sport.

A P-1 visa petition must include an advisory opinion from a labor organization with experience in the relevant area of entertainment or athletics. If no appropriate labor organization exists, USCIS may decide the petition without requiring an advisory opinion. If an advisory opinion is not submitted when it should be, USCIS will forward a copy of the petition and all supporting documentation to the national office of an appropriate labor organization within five days of the date of receipt of the petition for a response.

Multiple foreign nationals for an entertainment group or athletic team may be included on the same petition. Coaches and other support personnel require a separate petition. Separate petitions must be filed for P visa holders who are already in the United States and those who are outside the United States.

A P-1 foreign national is admitted to the United States for the duration of the time required to participate in the competition, event, or performance. A P-1 individual athlete may be admitted for up to five years.

Support Personnel

A P-1S visa is for foreign nationals coming to the United States to work in the capacity of essential support personnel for a P-1 athlete, team, or entertainment group. The P-1S visa is for a highly skilled, essential person who is an integral part of the performance of a P-1 athlete or entertainer by performing support services that cannot be readily performed by a United States worker and that are essential to the successful performance of the P-1 athlete or entertainer. Essential support personnel must have appropriate qualifications to perform the services, critical knowledge of the specific services to be performed, and experience in providing such support to the P-1 athlete or entertainer. Coaches, league officials, referees, front office personnel, camera operators, lighting technicians, and stage personnel are all examples of individuals who might be categorized as P-1S essential support personnel.

A P-1S visa petition requires a consultation from a labor organization, a statement describing the essential role, and a copy of the contract or summary of the oral agreement between the support personnel and the employer.

P-2 Visas

P-2 visas are for artists or entertainers, either individually or as a group, who enter the United States to perform in a reciprocal exchange program between an organization in the United States and an organization abroad that provides for the temporary exchange of artists or entertainers. Support personnel for a P-2 visa holder are also eligible to receive a P-2 visa.

P-3 Visas

P-3 visas are for artists or entertainers, either individually or as a group, who enter the United States to develop, interpret, represent, coach, or teach a unique or traditional ethnic, folk, cultural, musical, theatrical, or artistic performance or presentation. The event may be commercial or non-commercial but must be to further the understanding or development of the foreign national's art form.

7

Recommendation Letters and the Cover Letter

Recommendation Letters

It is unquestionable that the most important evidence presented to USCIS in support of an immigrant or nonimmigrant petition based on achievement is recommendation letters from past/current supervisors and independent experts in the field of achievement discussing the foreign national's past accomplishments and the impact of those accomplishments on the field as a whole. The immigration officer reading the letters and deciding whether to approve a petition is a layperson with no scientific/scholarly/artistic/business knowledge whatsoever. Most foreign nationals who write letters without attorney assistance write the letters like a journal article and the letters are overly technical and too difficult for the immigration officer to understand the exact nature of the accomplishments and why the accomplishments are important.

Recommendation letters should explain the following:

- What original contributions the foreign national has made to the field at all stages of his or her career;
- How others in the field have used the foreign national's work;
- What impact has the foreign national's accomplishments had (and will continue to have) on society, stressing its widespread impact and importance;
- How has the foreign national's work impacted the field;

- The foreign national's contributions must be explained in simple terms so that anyone can understand what the foreign national has accomplished and its practical significance;
- Why it is that the foreign national is one of that small percentage at the very top of the field (for extraordinary ability aliens);
- How the foreign national has received international recognition as outstanding (for outstanding professors and researchers);
- How the foreign national's accomplishments have had a degree of influence on the field as a whole above and beyond the substantial majority of others (for national interest waiver);
- What is the nature of the foreign national's current work and how will it benefit the United States; and
- What is the foreign national's record of success in the field.

The outline of a reference letter is as follows:

1. Introductory paragraph
2. Author provides background information about himself or herself
3. Author indicates how he or she knows (or does not know) the foreign national
4. Author discusses the foreign national's accomplishments
5. Conclusion

Successful recommendation letters:

- Go into detail about the original scientific/scholarly/artistic/ business contributions the foreign national has made;
- Explain the scientific/scholarly/artistic/business contributions in layperson's terms so the immigration officer reading the letter can understand what the foreign national has accomplished without any technical background;
- Explain how the foreign national's accomplishments have influenced the field as a whole by talking about the practical significance of the accomplishments and how the accomplishments are at the very top of the field, have received international recognition as outstanding, are above and beyond the work of the substantial majority of others in the field because of their major significance and groundbreaking nature; and

- Discuss the recognition conferred upon the foreign national's work such as where it was published, where it was presented at international conferences, how it was discussed by others, if it was patented, how it has been implemented in a clinical manner, etc.

Each and every one of the foreign national's accomplishments must be thoroughly discussed in detail in a simple way that an immigration officer can understand. The immigration officer reading the recommendation letters and deciding whether to grant a petition has no technical knowledge of the foreign national's field of expertise and knows nothing about it. The accomplishments must be explained in depth but in a way that anyone reading the letter can understand. Technical terms pertaining to the foreign national's field belong in the recommendation letters but each and every technical accomplishment must be explained in layperson's terms as if the foreign national was explaining his or her accomplishments to a class of fifth grade students. This type of analysis needs to be done for all of the foreign national's accomplishments throughout his or her entire career.

A recommendation letter needs to be a quick and easy read for anyone—not just someone with technical knowledge. In other words, the immigration officer needs to know exactly what the foreign national accomplished explained in easily understandable language, why what the foreign national accomplished is important, how what the foreign national accomplished influenced the field as a whole, and what national/international recognition the foreign national received for each accomplishment.

A recommendation letter must discuss each one of a foreign national's specific accomplishments in the field, then explain the accomplishment in simple terms, then talk about the importance of the accomplishment, then talk about the practical significance of the accomplishment (i.e., it identified a target for the development of a drug against liver cancer, etc.), then talk about how the accomplishment was recognized (i.e., specific publications, presentations, media articles, discussion by others, etc.). Each of the foreign national's significant accomplishments at all stages of the foreign national's career should be dissected according to this formula in chronological order.

Discussing all of the foreign national's accomplishments in chronological order helps the immigration officer read and understand all of the letters submitted as an entire group. Towards this end it is helpful for each recommendation letter to have a separate section/header for each significant accomplishment throughout the foreign national's entire career that led to recognition.

A recommendation letter must discuss the importance of the foreign national's accomplishments and explain why they are important. Most foreign nationals tend to provide the author with initial drafts of recommendation letters that are written on either an overly technical level or a very simplistic and general level that does not sufficiently describe the accomplishments with specificity. The letters must talk about the specific accomplishments the foreign national has made, what the foreign national's accomplishments mean in the real world, and why those accomplishments have influenced the field as a whole, represent major significant accomplishments, are among the top accomplishments ever made in the field, etc. The objective evidence of the importance of the foreign national's accomplishments (i.e., publications, presentations, etc.) needs to be discussed with specificity in relation to each accomplishment.

Some examples of how this is done are as follows:

> Dr. _____, an independent expert in the field from University of _____, states, "These findings were novel, **among the very top findings in the field,** and of widespread impact and importance as Dr. XXXXXX discovered a way to help the body not reject a transplanted organ." Dr. _____, an independent expert in the field of immunology from _____ Medical Center comments on Dr. XXXXXX's this work as following: "Dr. XXXXXX's findings were groundbreaking and above and beyond the work of others as he provided a tangible molecule for use as a drug to prevent transplant rejection."

> Dr. _____, states that "This was an important contribution to the field as it provided other scientists with a roadmap on

how to proceed to develop an HIV vaccine." Dr. _____, notes that "Through this work, I can conclude with certainty that Dr. XXXXXX conducted research that was significantly above and beyond the work of others in the field and established himself as **one of the best T-lymphocyte immunologists in the world.**"

Dr. _____, an independent expert in the field of immunology from University of _____, notes that "this is a finding of major impact and importance to the field" and "it provides a tangible drug target to fight infection and is a finding that is clearly above and beyond that of others in the field."

Dr. _____, an independent expert in the field from University of _____, provides the following comments on Dr. XXXXXX's work:

Thus, based upon Dr. XXXXXX's research, CD55, which can simultaneously control the complement immune system and T-lymphocyte immune response, has become a target for manipulation according to different situations to treat immune-related diseases. For example, in a situation of chronic virus infection, in which the host's T cell immunity is usually compromised, ways to remove or decrease the level of CD55 will elevate the complement activation level, and eventually promote T cell response to clear the invading virus. Correspondingly, in a situation of autoimmune disease where the body's immune system is hyper-active and attacking normal, healthy cells in the body, the level of CD55 can be increased to reduce the functioning of the immune system. Dr. XXXXXX's finding was of major impact and importance to the field on both national and international level as he provided a specific drug target to control the immune system. This is truly a revolutionary medical finding and sets Dr. XXXXXX apart from others in the field."

Dr. _____, notes that "this is a novel strategy that has had a major impact on the field since there are still not effective vaccines available for some contagious diseases like HIV infection."

Dr. _____,, an independent expert in the field from _____, University in the United Kingdom, calls the finding "of major significance to the field" and "relevant to the entire field of autoimmunity."

Dr. _____, an independent expert in the field from _____, University in Sweden, states the following about Dr. XXXXXX's DAF findings:

> In summary, this finding by Dr. XXXXXX was groundbreaking and of significant importance to understand and treat autoimmune diseases. As a result of Dr. XXXXXX's finding, DAF is now definitively a target for a drug to treat autoimmune disease. Suppressing the activities of both complement and T-lymphocyte cell immunities by increasing the amount of DAF on tissues is a strong and specific way to treat autoimmune disease and is superior compared to the currently used prevalent approaches whereby unselective immunosuppressive drugs are administered to patients which often cause severe side effects, such as hypertension, dyslipidemia and liver and kidney injury. This finding, published in the high impact international peer-reviewed *Journal of Immunology*, **is among the very top findings in the field of autoimmune disease** and sets Dr. XXXXXX apart from others in the field (emphasis added).

Dr. _____, notes that "this was a major significant finding as it provides a direct target (C3a and C5a) to treat autoimmune diseases."

Dr. _____, notes that "these findings were seminal observations in the field and among the **very top findings in the entire field**." These findings, also called "**among the top in the field**" by Dr. _____, were published by Dr. XXXXXX in *Blood*, which is among the highest-impact international journals.

Dr. _____, states, "This is the first report on the interaction between the complement system and the Toll-Like-Receptor system; and the <u>first proof anywhere in the world</u> to demonstrate the relationship between microorganism infection and autoimmune diseases. Because of Dr. XXXXXX's research, we now understand that one of the principal mechanisms of pathogen infection inducing autoimmune diseases is to promote the release of pro-inflammatory cytokines. This is a finding <u>far and above that of anyone else in the field</u> as Dr. XXXXXX has provided scientific findings that inhibiting excessive complement activation can prevent the high levels of pro-inflammatory cytokines that cause auto-immune diseases."

Dr. _____, summarizes Dr. XXXXXX's major research findings regarding how the complement system interacts with DAF and Toll-Like-Receptors as follows:

These novel discoveries by Dr. XXXXXX are clearly above and beyond the work of others as he discovered two principal mechanisms of complement activation that induce autoimmune diseases and suggested ways for clinically treating these diseases. **This clearly places him among the small percentage at the very top of**

the field. Considering the huge number of patients in the United States suffering from autoimmune diseases or disorders (The third most common category of disease in U.S.) Dr. XXXXXX's findings represent a **major milestone** in autoimmune disease research by providing an understanding of the role and action mechanisms of the complement system in autoimmune diseases. His findings provide a pathway for developing strategies to interrupt or cure these diseases.

Dr. _____, notes that "with these pioneering findings of Dr. XXXXXX in hand, scientists can now move to the next step on the road to devising safe and effective therapies and treatments for complement related autoimmune diseases," that "Dr. XXXXXX is an **immunologist at the very top of the field**" and that "the findings have been of widespread impact and importance at both the national and international level."

Examples of the type of language that should not be in a recommendation letter are as follows:

Our results indicate that (1) chronic ethanol diet did not increase the genome-wide binding activity of NF-κB at the baseline state with ~3200 target gene promoters; (2) PHx induced significant increase in NF-κB genome-wide binding at 1h, more so in chronic ethanol samples (5300 genes) than in controls (4000 genes). At 6h post PHx, only the control samples showed a further increase in NF-κB promoter binding ~5500 genes.

Numerous strong candidate genes like similar to GABA(A) receptor-associated protein like 2 (LOC683857), dynein, axonemal, heavy polypeptide 10 (Dnah10), dopamine receptor D5(Drd5), glutamate receptor, ionotropic kainate

2(Grik2), eukaryotic translation initiation factor 3, subunit E (Eif3e), cyclin-dependent kinase 17 (Cdk17), cyclin-dependent kinase 2-interacting protein (Cinp), melanoma antigen family B, 2 (Mageb2), SNARE homolog YKT6, member RAS oncogene family (RAB1B), corticotropin releasing hormone binding protein (Crhbp), nerve growth factor receptor (Ngfr), solute carrier family 6 (neurotransmitter transporter, taurine), member 6 (Slc6a6, acts as a sodium and chloride dependent taurine transporter plays a role in taurine transport; may play a role in neurotransmitter metabolism), synaptic vesicle glycoprotein 2c (Sv2c), similar to SNARE protein Ykt6 (RGD1562775), and postsynaptic membrane protein involved in excitatory synaptic transmission (Calsyntenin 2, Clstn2) etc have not been explained before, have been found in the significant QTL regions in his study.

For the author (and an immigration officer) the above paragraphs might as well have been written in a foreign language. The author could read the scientific terms in the above paragraphs a thousand times and still not understand them. It reads like a journal article and that is not what USCIS is looking for in a recommendation letter. USCIS does not care about the intricate technical details of a foreign national's accomplishments. This overly technical language does not help the immigration officer make a determination as to the foreign national's eligibility for a green card. A recommendation letter should provide a summary of what the foreign national accomplished, why what the foreign national accomplished is important and influenced the field, and how his or her accomplishments were recognized. Technical terms belong in the recommendation letters but all technical terms must be simply explained so that the recommendation letters do not sound like journal articles. It is also helpful to provide some general background information about the field in the recommendation letters to help the immigration officer understand the context of a foreign national's accomplishments.

Foreign nationals must keep in mind that they generally work in extremely technical fields that nobody in the general population understands. The goal of the recommendation letters is to help the foreign national be granted nonimmigrant status or a green card. To accomplish that goal the immigration officer needs to be able to easily read each recommendation letter as easily as they could read a newspaper article and understand exactly what the foreign national accomplished, exactly why what the foreign national accomplished is important, understand exactly how his or her accomplishments benefit health care, the economy, the environment, etc. from a practical standpoint, and understand exactly how the foreign national received recognition for each accomplishment.

In addition to the language not being overly technical, there is also no place in a recommendation letter for complimentary, superfluous language that is unsubstantiated. For example, language such as "Dr. X has a great work ethic" or "Dr. X is a nice person" adds nothing to USCIS making a determination of visa eligibility. The letters should also focus on how the foreign national's accomplishments have already impacted the field and avoid any speculation as to future influence. Language such as the finding of "Dr. X" has the "potential" to lead to a new drug or "may" improve disease diagnosis or has "great promise" for the development of personalized disease treatment should not be included in recommendation letters.

It is essential for the foreign national to obtain recommendation letters from independent experts in the field with whom the foreign national has not worked in addition to letters from colleagues and supervisors. Letters from colleagues who have worked at the same institution as the foreign national and the foreign national's supervisors do not carry much weight because USCIS expects colleagues and supervisors to speak positively about the foreign national's research. For this reason, in recommendation letters from colleagues and supervisors the author usually just has that individual discuss the accomplishments the foreign national made at the particular employer/institution/organization where the foreign national worked with the colleague/supervisor.

The author generally advises foreign nationals to obtain a letter from each of their prior supervisors and then to obtain four to six independent letters from experts in their field with whom they have not previously worked and who do not know them personally but who are aware of the foreign national's accomplishments in the field. Foreign nationals generally find independent experts by asking their colleagues for recommendations or by contacting individuals who they have met at conferences or who have referenced the foreign national's accomplishments in their own work. The quality of the independent letters is more influential than the quantity.

The author of a recommendation letter should be qualified to make an objective and credible assessment of the foreign national's accomplishments. Letters obtained from independent experts both in the United States and internationally help demonstrate the widespread impact of the foreign national's accomplishments. The reputation/standing in the field of the independent expert is not as important as the content of the letter and that the independent expert came to know about the foreign national's work through reputation. The independent expert letters can demonstrate that the author has knowledge of the foreign national through reputation by indicating that the author has never met the foreign national, has read the foreign national's publications in the course of his or her own work, has utilized the foreign national's original accomplishments, etc.

The *curriculum vitae* of the author of a recommendation letter should not be submitted to USCIS as the focus of the evaluation should be on the foreign national, not the author. The author providing background about his or her credentials within the body of the letter is the appropriate way to qualify the author as an expert. The letter should be dated, placed on the author's business letterhead, and signed by the author. If the author is not permitted to place the letter on business letterhead it may be placed on plain paper and if possible the author could provide an explanation as to why the letter is not being provided on business letterhead and/or evidence of the author's employment such as a business card. USCIS does not require the original letter and it is sufficient to submit a copy of the letter.

The foreign national should provide the content for the recommendation letters. The foreign national is the person who knows his or her accomplishments best and can best explain the complex aspects of those accomplishments in simple terms and best explain the practical significance of his or her accomplishments. An attorney does not have the knowledge to sufficiently explain the foreign national's accomplishments and their impact on the field as a whole in a non-technical manner. An attorney cannot provide the content for the recommendation letters from scratch because an attorney does not know and does not understand the nature of the foreign national's accomplishments. The role of the attorney, which is a role of critical importance, is to provide sample recommendation letters, make suggestions regarding the content of the letters, ensure proper English and grammar in the letters, and help write the letters so they properly discuss the nature and importance of the foreign national's accomplishments and how those accomplishments qualify the foreign national for the classification sought in a manner that is understandable to the immigration officer adjudicating the petition.

The foreign national wants the immigration officer who reads the recommendation letters submitted with the petition and who is deciding whether to approve the petition to be able to easily understand the recommendation letters and say, "I want this individual in the United States doing the work that they do to benefit the United States." The way to have the best possible chance of making that happen is for the foreign national to provide the content for the recommendation letters.

The Cover Letter

The cover letter submitted to USCIS must explain how the foreign national meets the legal requirements to receive approval in the category in which the foreign national is applying. For example, the legal standards for EB-1A extraordinary ability aliens, EB-1B outstanding professors and researchers, and EB-2 national interest waiver are all different and the cover letter must be tailored to each individual category.

The attorney cover letter submitted by the author on behalf of clients does the following:

- Sets forth the category in which the foreign national is applying and how the foreign national meets the legal requirements for approval in the category

- Provides background information about the foreign national's field of expertise so the immigration officer understands the context of the foreign national's accomplishments
- Summarizes each of the foreign national's accomplishments, the importance of each accomplishment, and the recognition conferred upon the foreign national for each accomplishment
- Identifies the evidence being submitted in support of the petition and how that evidence satisfies the legal requirements for approval

It is critical to explain to the immigration officer in the cover letter why the foreign national is legally eligible to receive petition approval based on past achievement. The cover letter should be organized in a manner that clearly sets forth how the evidence being submitted in support of the petition qualifies the foreign national for approval in the requested classification.

8

Premium Processing

The USCIS premium processing service involves paying an extra fee to have a petition decided within fifteen calendar days. If USCIS does not process the petition within that time frame, USCIS will refund the premium processing service fee and the case will continue to receive expedited processing. In practice, USCIS generally processes all premium processing cases within the fifteen-calendar-day period.

The fifteen-calendar-day period begins when USCIS receives Form I-907 with the required premium processing service fee. Form I-907 can either be filed simultaneously with the petition or a petition filed via regular processing can be upgraded to premium processing service at any time while the petition is pending by filing Form I-907 with the required premium processing service fee. Foreign nationals who wish to use the USCIS premium processing service must send Form I-907 (and the underlying petition if filed simultaneously with Form I-907) to a special premium processing address, which varies depending on the work location and the type of petition for which the premium processing service is requested.

The O and P achievement-based nonimmigrant petitions are eligible for the premium processing service.

The EB-1A extraordinary ability aliens and EB-1B outstanding professors and researchers achievement-based immigrant petitions are eligible for the premium processing service.

The EB-2 national interest waiver achievement-based immigrant petition is not eligible for the premium processing service.

Only the petitioner or the petitioner's representative may file a request for premium processing service. Thus, for O and P nonimmigrant and EB-1B outstanding professors and researchers immigrant petitions that require an employer sponsor, only the employer or the employer's representative may file the request for premium processing service. For an EB-1A extraordinary ability aliens achievement-based immigrant petition where the foreign national is typically self-filing, the foreign national or the foreign national's representative may file a request for premium processing service. There are no regulations regarding payment of the premium processing service fee for the achievement-based petitions discussed in this book, so any party may pay the premium processing service fee for an achievement-based petition.

Within the fifteen-calendar-day period USCIS will issue an approval notice, a denial notice, a notice of intent to deny, a request for evidence, or open an investigation for fraud or misrepresentation. If the petition requires the submission of additional evidence or a response to a notice of intent to deny, a new fifteen-calendar-day period will begin upon receipt by USCIS of a complete response to the request for evidence or notice of intent to deny.

There are multiple factors to consider when deciding whether to utilize the premium processing service.

In the O and P nonimmigrant context, the foreign national should check the current USCIS processing times as regular processing times for these types of petitions can be as little as two weeks, which makes premium processing unnecessary. Additionally, the filing of an extension of status petition in the O and P categories extends the foreign national's work authorization for a period of 240 days pending a decision on the extension petition so the premium processing service is generally not necessary for O and P extension of status requests.

If regular USCIS processing time is running longer than two weeks, then the premium processing service may be necessary to ensure timely approval of an O or P nonimmigrant petition if the foreign national must begin work by a certain date. The premium processing service may also be necessary in the O context if an individual is nearing the six-year maximum of allowable time in H-1B status without the ability to extend H-1B status beyond six years and wishes to change to O status without a lapse in employment. Another example in which premium processing may be beneficial for an O or P nonimmigrant petition is if the foreign national is filing an extension of status petition and has an urgent need to travel outside the United States and needs an approved petition to apply for a visa at a United States embassy overseas to return to the United States following foreign travel.

Most of the author's clients elect to utilize the premium processing service when filing an EB-1A extraordinary ability aliens or EB-1B outstanding professors and researchers achievement-based immigrant petition. The reason is based on risk aversion. Although it is legally permissible to file an I-485 application for adjustment of status (i.e., green card application) simultaneously with an EB-1A or EB-1B I-140 petition, if the I-140 petition is denied then the I-485 application of the principal applicant and any derivative spouse and/or child will also be denied and the filing fees and medical examination fees associated with the I-485 application(s) will be lost. Additionally, if anyone with a pending I-485 application utilized an employment authorization document to work for an employer that was not permitted by the underlying nonimmigrant status, or if the underlying nonimmigrant status is expired at the time of the denial of the I-485 application, then such denial will result in the foreign national and/or derivative family members being unlawfully present in the United States. By utilizing the premium processing service, if the I-140 petition is approved in fifteen calendar days or less then the foreign national and any derivative family members may thereafter file I-485 green card applications quickly without the aforementioned risks. Since it can take four months or longer to receive a decision on an EB-1A or EB-1B petition without the use of the premium processing service, a foreign national who does not want to take the risk of filing the I-485 application simultaneously with the I-140 petition will receive the green card at least four months sooner by utilizing the premium processing service than a foreign national who does not want to take the risk of filing the I-485 application simultaneously with the I-140 petition and does not want to utilize the premium processing service.

Finally, foreign nationals filing in the EB-1A and EB-1B categories often utilize the premium processing service simply because they do not want to wait months to find out whether or not a petition will be approved paving the way for a successful green card application.

9

Employment-Based Immigrant Visa Availability: China and India versus the Rest of the World

The Immigration and Nationality Act limits the number of employment-based preference visas to 140,000 per year and these numbers are allocated among the various employment-based preference categories. Furthermore, each country in the world, regardless of population size, cannot receive more than 7 percent of the 140,000 employment-based green cards, which are 9,800 per country.

The 140,000 employment-based preference visas are divided among the various preference categories as follows:

EB-1 Priority Workers = 28.6 percent of the 140,000 visas plus any numbers not required for the EB-4 and EB-5 preferences. Each country thus gets 9,800 x 28.6 percent = 2802 + numbers not used in EB-4 and EB-5.

EB-2 Professionals with Advanced Degrees or Persons with Exceptional Ability (Including National Interest Waiver Petitions) = 28.6 percent of the 140,000 visas plus any numbers not required for the EB-1 preference. Each country thus gets 9,800 x 28.6 percent = 2802 + numbers not used in EB-1.

EB-3 Skilled or Professional Workers = 28.6 percent of the 140,000 visas plus any numbers not required for the EB-1 and EB-2 preferences, not more than 10,000 of which are for "other workers." Each country thus gets 9,800 x 28.6 percent = 2802 + numbers not used in EB-2.

EB-4 Special Immigrants = 7.1 percent of the 140,000 visas. Each country thus gets 9,800 x 7.1 percent = 695.

EB-5 Investors = 7.1 percent of the 140,000 visas, 3,000 of which are for investors in a targeted rural or high-unemployment area and 3,000 of which are for investors in regional centers. Each country thus gets 9,800 x 7.1 percent = 695.

Most countries in the world never reach their per-country limit in the employment-based preference categories. However, more than 9,800 foreign nationals from China and more than 9,800 foreign nationals from India want to immigrate to the United States each year in the employment-based preference categories.

Due to the high credentials required for approval as an EB-1A extraordinary ability alien or an EB-1B outstanding professor/researcher, China and India almost never reach the per-country limitation in the EB-1 priority worker category and visa numbers in the EB-1 priority worker category are almost always available. However, the per-country limitations in the EB-2 and EB-3 categories are almost always reached each year for China and India, meaning there is a backlog and foreign nationals from China and India must usually wait many years to apply for and receive their green cards in the EB-2 and EB-3 categories. For example, an individual born in India and eligible to apply for an immigrant visa in the EB-3 category can face a backlog of more than ten years before a green card application can be filed. This is why the EB-1 priority worker category is so highly desired by foreign nationals from China and India. Additionally, for all countries worldwide the supply of employment-based visa numbers exceeds demand in the EB-3 category.

Due to the high credentials required for approval as an EB-1A extraordinary ability alien or an EB-1B outstanding professor/researcher, foreign nationals from China and India who do not meet such credentials must strategize. In such a situation, eligible foreign nationals from China and India are advised to file an EB-2 national interest waiver petition while improving on their credentials and achievements for EB-1A/EB-1B, or for EB-1B to obtain the required three years of teaching/research experience, secure a permanent job offer as a professor or researcher, and/or obtain employer sponsorship. Such a strategy allows foreign nationals from China and India to establish a priority date in the EB-2 category, to enable the extension of H-1B status beyond the six-year limit if the national interest waiver petition is approved, and to improve the credentials required to receive an approved EB-1 petition where visa numbers are current. Filing an EB-2 national interest waiver petition and then working to establish the credentials, employer sponsorship, and so on necessary for EB-1A/EB-1B approval has many benefits.

Visa numbers are based on country of birth, regardless of current citizenship. However, there are certain exceptions to this rule, the most common of which is if the foreign national's spouse was born in another country that is not subject to a visa, the foreign national can utilize "cross chargeability" and utilize the employment-based visa numbers in the spouse's country of birth.

When the demand for employment-based visas exceeds the supply, green card issuances are "backlogged" or "retrogressed" to a priority date in the past, which is known as the "cut-off" date. The priority date is established by either filing an I-140 immigrant petition for alien worker or a PERM Labor Certification Application. The "cut-off date" is the date that the United States Department of State (DOS) is currently allocating employment-based visa numbers to a specific category and country. Only when a foreign national's priority date is on or before the cut-off date is application for and issuance of a green card possible.

Each month the DOS publishes a *Visa Bulletin* containing the visa availability for individuals seeking family and employment-based United States permanent resident status. The *Visa Bulletin* is used by United States consulates and embassies worldwide to determine whether to issue immigrant visas and by USCIS to determine whether a Form I-485 application to register permanent residence or adjust status (i.e., green card application) may be accepted for filing or adjudicated.

The *Visa Bulletin* is generally issued on or around the eighth day of each month and contains the data be used to govern immigrant visa issuance for the following month. The current *Visa Bulletin*, as well as past *Visa Bulletins*, can be found on the DOS website.

The cut-off dates listed in the *Visa Bulletin* change each month and generally tend to move forward as the DOS and USCIS adjudicate pending cases and clear the backlog. However, movement varies among EB categories and among countries and the dates do not always move forward. On a monthly basis, if supply exceeds demand for a particular employment preference visa category for country of birth or country of visa chargeability, immigrant visas are deemed current and are designated as such in the report with a letter "C." This means that immigrant visa numbers are available for individuals with approved I-140 petitions in that particular visa preference category and country of birth or country of visa chargeability. If demand exceeds supply for a particular employment preference visa category for country of birth or country of visa chargeability, that category is classified as "oversubscribed" and the DOS must impose a cut-off date. Under such circumstances, only applicants who have a priority date earlier than the date listed in the *Visa Bulletin* may have an immigrant visa number available to apply for and/or be issued a green card.

In some instances, a priority date listed as current in the *Visa Bulletin* one month will not be current the next month or will have an earlier priority date the next month. This is known as visa retrogression and most often occurs when the annual limit on immigrant visas has been reached. When a new fiscal year begins on October 1, a new supply of visa numbers becomes available and usually (but not always) returns visa cut-off dates to where they were before retrogression occurred. Forward visa movement also tends to happen during the last few months of a fiscal year (June, July, August, September) as the various government agencies make an effort to use up the prior year's allotment before the new allotment becomes available, as unused visa numbers in a fiscal year cannot be recaptured in a subsequent year.

Another factor contributing to employment-based visa backlogs is that the application of a derivative spouse or child counts against the 140,000 annual number of visas, which accounts for approximately 80,000 of the 140,000 visas.

It is imperative that foreign nationals in the United States awaiting the availability of an immigrant visa number maintain nonimmigrant status until the priority date becomes current to be able to proceed to adjustment of status or immigrant visa processing. There are provisions in place to allow a foreign national to extend H-1B status beyond the six-year maximum allowable stay in H-1B status plus the recapture of time the foreign national spent outside the United States while in H-1B status in one year increments if a PERM Labor Certification Application or I-140 immigrant petition for alien worker was filed more than 365 days in advance of the six-year maximum allowable stay in H-1B status plus the recapture of time the foreign national spent outside the United States while in H-1B status. There are also provisions in place to allow a foreign national to extend H-1B status in three year increments beyond the six-year maximum allowable stay in H-1B status plus the recapture of time the foreign national spent outside the United States if there is an approved I-140 immigrant petition for alien worker but the foreign national cannot file for a green card because of immigrant visa backlogs.

10

Frequently Asked Questions

Q: **What is the Difference Between an Immigrant Work Visa and a Nonimmigrant Work Visa?**

A: An immigrant visa is for a foreign national to live and work permanently in the United States whereas a nonimmigrant visa is for a foreign national to live and work temporarily in the United States.

Q: **Do I need an Employer Sponsor for a Work Visa?**

A: All temporary nonimmigrant work visas require employer sponsorship. Immigrant work visas can be self-filed by a foreign national in the EB-1A extraordinary ability aliens and EB-2 national interest waiver categories. All other immigrant work visas require an employer sponsor.

Q: **Do I have to have an attorney?**

A: In a word—no. If you choose to proceed without legal representation you may. However, as indicated in this book the legal requirements for immigrant and nonimmigrant work visas based on achievement are very high and it is recommend that a foreign national utilize the expertise of a qualified immigration attorney in preparing and submitting the evidence in support of a petition filed with USCIS.

Q: **What are the different classifications to apply for an Immigrant Visa or a Nonimmigrant Visa based on achievement?**

A: The general classifications to apply for an immigrant visa based on achievement are EB-1A extraordinary ability aliens, EB-1B outstanding professors and researchers, and EB-2 national interest waiver. The general classifications to apply for a nonimmigrant visa based on achievement are the O-1 visa for extraordinary ability aliens and the P visa for athletes, artists, and entertainers.

Q: What are the requirements for approval in the EB-1A Extraordinary Ability Aliens Classification?

A: The EB-1A extraordinary ability aliens classification is for foreign nationals with extraordinary ability in the sciences, arts, education, business, or athletics. Individuals must demonstrate that they have sustained national or international acclaim and that their achievements have been recognized in the field of expertise, indicating that they are one of that small percentage who has risen to the very top of their field of endeavor. They must plan to continue to work in their area of extraordinary ability and must substantially benefit prospectively the United States.

Q: What are the requirements for approval in the EB-1B Outstanding Professors and Researchers Classification?

A: The EB-1B outstanding professors and researchers classification is for foreign nationals who are internationally recognized as outstanding in a specific academic field. EB-1B requires that the foreign national have a full-time permanent job offer in the United States in the academic field at a university (for professors or researchers) or a qualifying private employer (for researchers) and at least three years of teaching and/or research experience in the academic field.

Q: What are the requirements for approval in the EB-2 National Interest Waiver Classification?

A: The EB-2 national interest waiver classification is for foreign nationals who possess an advanced degree (i.e., a master's degree or higher), or exceptional ability in the sciences, arts, or business. The foreign national must seek to work in an area of "substantial intrinsic merit," the benefit of the foreign national's proposed activity must be "national in scope," and the foreign national must demonstrate a "track record of success" "with some degree of influence on the field as a whole" above and beyond the substantial majority of others in the field. The EB-2 national interest waiver classification is also available for qualified entrepreneurs.

Q: What are the requirements for approval for an O-1 Visa?

A: The O-1 visa is a temporary work visa available to those foreign nationals who have "extraordinary ability in the sciences, arts, education, business or athletics" that "has been demonstrated by sustained national or international acclaim." An O-1 visa requires a consultation.

Q: What are the requirements for approval for a P Visa?

A: P-1 visas are for a foreign national who is a member of an entertainment group with an international reputation that is coming to the United States to perform or is an athlete with international recognition or who is part of a team with international recognition coming to the United States to compete individually or as part of a team in a specific athletic competition. P-2 visas are for artists or entertainers, either individually or as a group, who enter the United States to perform in a reciprocal exchange program between an organization in the United States and an organization abroad that provides for the temporary exchange of artists or entertainers. P-3 visas are for artists or entertainers, either individually or as a group, who enter the United States to develop, interpret, represent, coach, or teach a unique or traditional ethnic, folk, cultural, musical, theatrical, or artistic performance or presentation. The event may be commercial or non-commercial but must be to further the understanding or development of the foreign national's art form. A P visa requires a consultation.

Q: What constitutes a successful recommendation letter?

A: A recommendation letter should discuss each one of a foreign national's specific accomplishments in the field, then explain the accomplishment in simple terms, then talk about the importance of the accomplishment, then talk about the practical significance of the accomplishment, then talk about how the accomplishment was recognized.

Q: What constitutes a successful cover letter?

A: A cover letter submitted to USCIS must explain how the foreign national meets the legal requirements to receive approval in the category in which the foreign national is applying. The cover letter sets forth how the evidence submitted in support of the petition legally qualifies the foreign national for approval in the requested classification.

Q: Should I utilize the premium processing service?

A: In the immigrant visa context, premium processing is only available in the EB-1A extraordinary ability aliens and EB-1B outstanding professors and researchers categories; not the EB-2 national interest waiver category. In the nonimmigrant visa context, premium processing is available in both the O-1 and P visa categories. Whether to utilize the premium processing service is a decision made on a case-by-case basis based on the specific circumstances/preferences of the foreign national. In the immigrant visa context, most foreign nationals utilize premium processing when filing in the EB-1A or EB-1B category.

Q: What if I am from China or India?

A: Foreign nationals from China and India are subject to an extensive wait of many years to receive a green card in the EB-2 and EB-3 categories. For that reason if a foreign national from China or India may be eligible for approval in either the EB-1A extraordinary ability aliens category or the EB-1B outstanding professors and researchers category a petition in one of those categories should be explored.

ABOUT THE AUTHOR

Brian H. Getson leads the nationwide immigration practice of Getson & Schatz PC (www.click4immigraton.com) with offices in Philadelphia, PA and New York, NY; and has extensive experience representing scientific researchers and other foreign nationals of achievement in filing petitions with United States Citizenship and Immigration Services in the EB-1A extraordinary ability aliens, EB-1B outstanding professors and researchers, EB-2 national interest waiver, O-1, and P visa categories.

Mr. Getson is a member of the American Immigration Lawyer's Association, has lectured to other immigration lawyers at continuing legal education seminars, and has authored media articles and books on immigration. Mr. Getson may be reached by phone at 215-520-4000 or via e-mail at bgetson@getsonimmigration.com.

ASPATORE